GERMAN

in 10 minutes a day™

by **Kristine Kershul,** M.A., University of California, Santa Barbara

Published by
Bilingual Books, Inc.
5903 Seaview Avenue N.W.
Seattle, Washington 98107, U.S.A.
Telephone: (206) 789-7544
Telex: 499 6629 BBKS UI

Distributed by
USA: Cliffs Notes, Inc., Box 80728, Lincoln, Nebraska 68501
UK: Ruskin Book Services, 15 Comberton Hill, Kidderminster, Worcestershire DY10 1QG
 Sixth edition: printed 1985
(ISBN 0-916682-99-4)

(ahl-fah-bate) das Alphabet

Many German letters sound the same as in English, but some German letters are pronounced or written differently. To learn the German sounds of these letters, write each example in the space provided. After you practice each word, see if you can locate it on the map.

German letter	English sound	Example	*Write it here*
a	ah	**Hamburg** *(hahm-boorg)*	
ä	ay	**Dänemark** *(day-nah-mark)*	
au	ow/au	**Passau** *(pahs-sau)*	*Passau*
äu/eu	oy	**Europa** *(oy-roh-pah)*	
ch	hk *(breathe hard)*	**Frankreich** *(frahnk-reihk)*	
e *(varies)*	ay *or* eh	**Bremen** *(bray-men)*	
ei	eye/ai/i	**Rhein** *(rine)*	
er	air	**Berlin** *(bair-leen)*	
i	ih	**Inn** *(in)*	
ie	ee	**Kiel** *(keel)*	
o	oh	**Polen** *(poh-len)*	
ö	ur	**Köln** *(kurln)*	
qu	kv	**Marquartstein** *(mar-kvart-shtine)*	
r	*(slightly rolled)*	**Rostock** *(roh-shtoke)*	
s *(varies)*	s *or* z	**Ostsee** *(ohst-zay)*	
sch	sh	**Schweden** *(shvay-den)*	
ß	ss	**Meßstetten** *(mess-shtet-en)*	
th	t	**Gotha** *(go-tah)*	
u	oo	**Ulm** *(oolm)*	*Ulm*
ü	ew/ue	**München** *(meun-shen)*	
v	f	**Hannover** *(hahn-noh-fair)*	
w	v	**Weimar** *(vie-mar)*	
z	ts	**Koblenz** *(koh-blents)*	
e *(end of word)*	ah	**Elbe** *(el-bah)*	

Now practice the important words you learned on the inside front cover.

Seven Key Question Words

Step 1

When you arrive in the **Bundesrepublik** *(boon-des-ray-poo-bleek)* Federal Republic **Deutschland,** *(doych-lahnt)* Germany the very first thing you will need to do is to ask questions— "Where is the train station?" "Where can I exchange money?" "Where (**wo**) *(voh)* is the lavatory?" "**Wo** is a restaurant?" "**Wo** do I catch a taxi?" "**Wo** is a good hotel?" "**Wo** is my luggage?"—and the list will go on and on for the entire length of your visit. In German, there are SEVEN KEY QUESTION WORDS to learn. For example, the seven key question words will help you to find out exactly what you are ordering in a restaurant before you order it—and not after the surprise (or shock!) arrives. These seven basic question words all begin with "**w**" (which is pronounced like "v").

Take a few minutes to study and practice saying the seven basic question words listed below. Then cover the German words with your hand and fill in each of the blanks with the matching German **Wort** *(vort)* word.

1.	*(voh)* **WO**	=	WHERE	wo, wo, wo, wo
2.	*(vahs)* **WAS**	=	WHAT	______
3.	*(vair)* **WER**	=	WHO	______
4.	*(vah-room)* **WARUM**	=	WHY	______
5.	*(vahn)* **WANN**	=	WHEN	______
6.	*(vee)* **WIE**	=	HOW	______
7.	*(vee-feel)* **WIEVIEL**	=	HOW MUCH	______

Now test yourself to see if you really can keep these *(vur-tair)* **Wörter** (words) straight in your mind. Draw lines between the German *(oont)* **und** (and) English equivalents below.

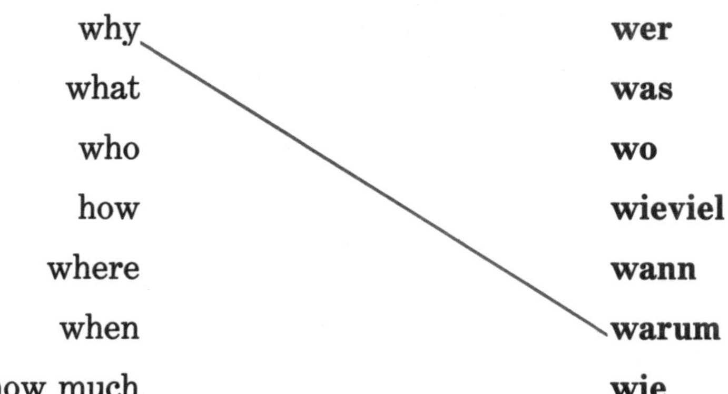

why	**wer**
what	**was**
who	**wo**
how	**wieviel**
where	**wann**
when	**warum**
how much	**wie**

Examine the following questions containing these *(vur-tair)* **Wörter**. Practice the sentences out loud *(oont)* **und** then quiz yourself by filling in the blanks below with the correct question *(vort)* **Wort**.

(voh) (ist) (ine) (tay-lay-fohn)
Wo ist ein Telefon?
Where is a telephone?

(vair) (dahs)
Wer ist das?
Who is that?

(vahn) (kohmt) (dair) (tsook)
Wann kommt der Zug?
When comes the train?

(vee-feel) (koh-stet)
Wieviel kostet das?
How much costs this?

(vahs) (lohs)
Was ist los?
What is wrong?

(vee) (dair) (zah-laht)
Wie ist der Salat?
How is the salad?

(vahn) (kohmt) (mahn)
Wann kommt der Mann?
When comes the man?

(vah-room) (neehkt)
Warum kommt der Zug nicht?
Why comes the train not?

1. ____________ **ist der Salat?**
2. ____________ **kostet das?**
3. ____________ **ist los?**
4. ____________ **ist ein Telefon?**
5. ____________ **kommt der Zug nicht?**
6. Wer **ist das?**
7. ____________ **kommt der Zug?**
8. ____________ **kommt der Mann?**

(voh) **Wo** will be your most used question *(vort)* **Wort** so let's concentrate on it. Say each of the following German sentences aloud. Then write out each sentence without looking at the example. If you don't succeed on the first try, don't give up. Just practice each sentence until you are able to do it easily.

Don't forget that you pronounce "**ei**" like "eye" **und** "**ie**" like "ee." Also, in German you pronounce every letter you see.

Wo *(voh)* **ist eine** *(ine-ah)* **Toilette?** *(toy-let-tah)*

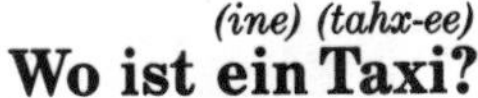

Wo ist ein *(ine)* **Taxi?** *(tahx-ee)*

Wo ist ein Bus? *(boos)*

____________________ ____________________

Wo ist ein Restaurant? *(res-toh-rahnt)*

Wo ist eine *(ine-ah)* **Bank?** *(bahnk)*

Wo ist ein *(ine)* **Hotel?**

____________________ ____________________ ____________________

Ja, *(yah)* yes, many of the **Wörter** *(vur-tair)* which look like **Englisch** *(eng-leash)* English are also **Deutsch.** *(doych)* German. Since **Deutsch und** *(oont)* **Englisch** are related languages, your work here **ist** simpler. You will be amazed at the number of **Wörter** which are identical (or almost identical). Of course, they do not always sound the same when spoken by a German, but the similarity will certainly surprise you. Listed below are five "free" **Wörter** beginning with "A" to help you get started. Be sure to say each **Wort** *(vort)* aloud **und** *(oont)* then write out the German **Wort** in the blank to the right.

☐ **die Adresse** *(ah-dress-sah)*............	the address	____________
☐ **das Amerika** *(ah-mair-ih-kah)*.........	America	____________
☐ **der April** *(ah-pril)*..................	April	____________
☐ **der August** *(ow-goost)*................	August	____________
☐ **das Auto** *(ow-toh)*....................	the car/automobile	____________

Free **Wörter** like these will appear at the bottom of the following pages in a yellow color band. Check them off as you learn them. They are easy—enjoy them!

Step 2

"the"

All of these words mean "the" *(owf)* **auf** *(doych)* **Deutsch** (German)**:**

(dair) **der**	*(dee)* **die**	*(dahs)* **das**	*(dain)* **den**	*(dehm)* **dem**	*(des)* **des**

(mahn) **der Mann:**	the man	*(fah-tair)* **den Vater:**	the father
(frow) **die Frau:**	the woman	*(froy-line)* **dem Fräulein:**	the young woman
(kint) **das Kind:**	the child	*(ow-toes)* **des Autos:**	the car

"a" or "an"

All of these words mean "a" or "an":

(ine) **ein**	*(ine-ah)* **eine**	*(ine-in)* **einen**	*(ine-air)* **einer**	*(ine-em)* **einem**	*(ine-es)* **eines**

ein Mann:	a man	**einem Vater:**	a father
eine Frau:	a woman	**einem Fräulein:**	a young girl
ein Kind:	a child	**eines Autos:**	a car

(doych) **Deutsch** (German) has multiple *(vur-tair)* **Wörter** for "the" *(oont)* **und** "a," but there **ist** no need to worry about it. Just make a choice **und** remember to use one of these **Wörter** when you mean "the" *(oh-dair)* **oder** (or) "a."

Step 3

die *(ding-ah)* Dinge (things)

Before you proceed **mit** (with) this step, situate yourself comfortably in your living room. Now look around you. Can you name the things which you see in this *(tsi-mair)* **Zimmer** (room) in German? Probably you can guess *(dahs) (zoh-fah)* **das Sofa** and maybe even *(dee) (lahm-pah)* **die Lampe**. Let's learn the rest of them. After practicing these *(vur-tair)* **Wörter** out loud, write them in the blanks below **und** on the next page.

(bilt) **das Bild** = the picture das Bild

(dee) (deck-ah) **die Decke** = the ceiling ____________

☑ **der Amerikaner** *(ah-mair-ih-kahn-air)*. . the American ____________
☐ **der Apfel** *(ahp-fel)*. . . . . the apple ____________
☐ **der Appetit** *(ah-pe-teet)*. . . . . the appetite ____________
☐ **der Akzent** *(ahk-tsent)*. . . . . the accent ____________
☐ **das Afrika** *(ah-fri-kah)*. . . . . Africa ____________

(dee) (eck-ah)
die Ecke = the corner ______________________

(dahs) (fen-stair)
das Fenster = the window ______________________

(lahm-pah)
die Lampe = the lamp ______________________

(leeht)
das Licht = the light ______________________

(zoh-fah)
das Sofa = the sofa ______________________

(dair) (shtool)
der Stuhl = the chair ______________________

(tep-eeh)
der Teppich = the carpet ______________________

(tish)
der Tisch = the table ______________________

(tewr)
die Tür = the door die Tür

(uhr)
die Uhr = the clock ______________________

(for-hahng)
der Vorhang = the curtain ______________________

(vahnt)
die Wand = the wall ______________________

You will notice that the correct form of *(dair) (dee) (oh-dair)(dahs)* **der, die, oder das** is given **mit** (with) each noun. This is for your information—just remember to use one of them. Open your book to the sticky labels (between pages 48 and 49). Peel off the first 14 labels **und** proceed around the *(tsi-mair)* **Zimmer,** labeling these items in your home. This will help to increase your *(doy-chah)* **deutsche Wort** power easily. Don't forget to say **das** *(vort)* **Wort** as you attach each label.

Now ask yourself, *(voh)* *(bilt)* **„Wo ist das Bild?"** **und** point at it while you answer, **„Dort** (there) **ist das Bild."** Continue on down the list until you feel comfortable with these new **Wörter**. Say, "**Wo ist** *(dee)* **die Decke**?" Then reply, "**Dort ist die Decke**," and so on. When you can identify all the items on the list, you will be ready to move on.

Now, starting on the next page, let's learn some basic parts of the house.

- ☐ **der Akt** *(ahkt)*.................... act (of a play) ______________
- ☐ **die Akademie** *(ah-kah-dih-mee)*........ the academy ______________
- ☐ **der Alkohol** *(ahl-koh-hole)*............ the alcohol ______________
- ☐ **alle** *(ahl-lah)*........................ all ______________
- ☐ **der Autor** *(ow-tohr)*.................. the author ______________

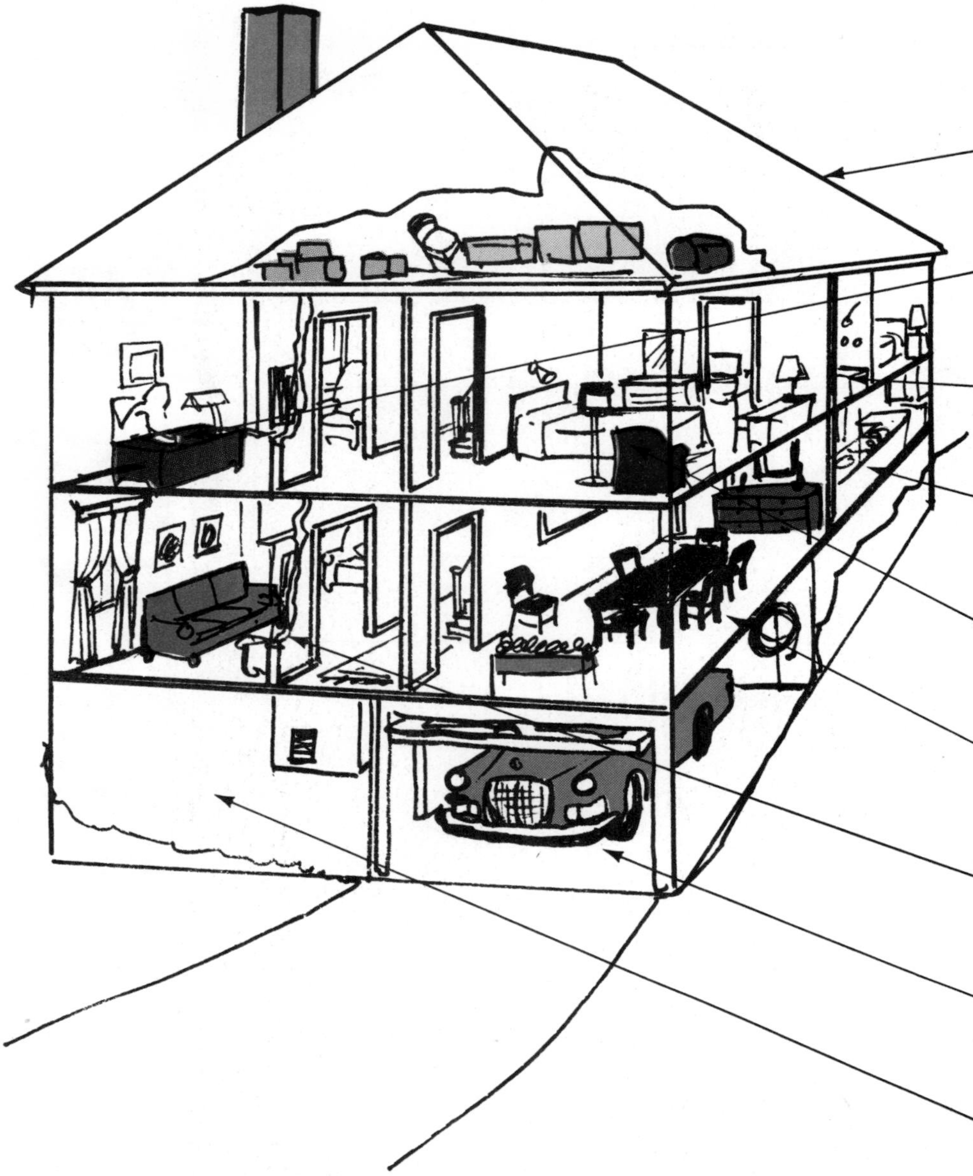

(house)
das Haus = the house
(house)
Dort ist das Haus.

(bew-roh)
das Büro
office / study

(bah-da-tsi-mair)
das Badezimmer
bathroom

(kew-sha)
die Küche
kitchen

(shlahf-tsi-mair)
das Schlafzimmer
bedroom

(es-tsi-mair)
das Eßzimmer
dining room

(vohn-tsi-mair)
das Wohnzimmer
living room

(ga-rah-zha)
die Garage
garage

(kel-lair)
der Keller
basement

While learning these new *(vur-tair)* **Wörter,** let's not forget

(ow-toe) *(vah-gen)*
das Auto / der Wagen

(fahr-raht)
das Fahrrad

(hoont)
der Hund

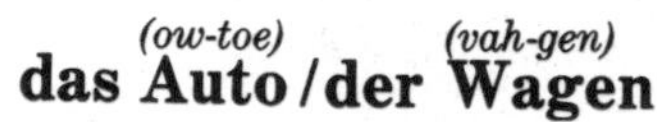

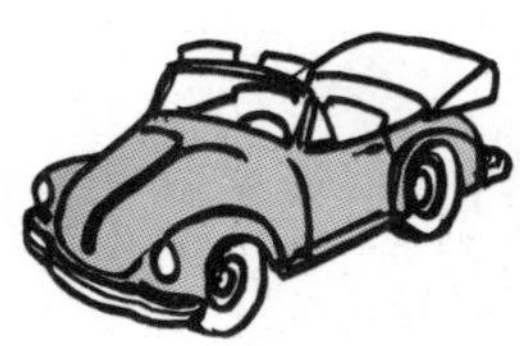

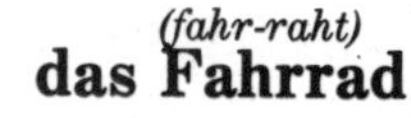

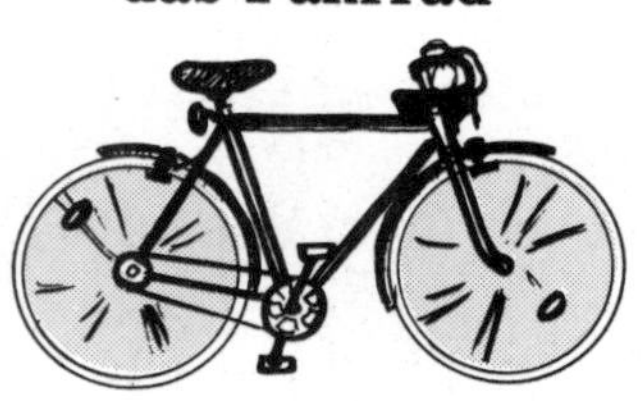

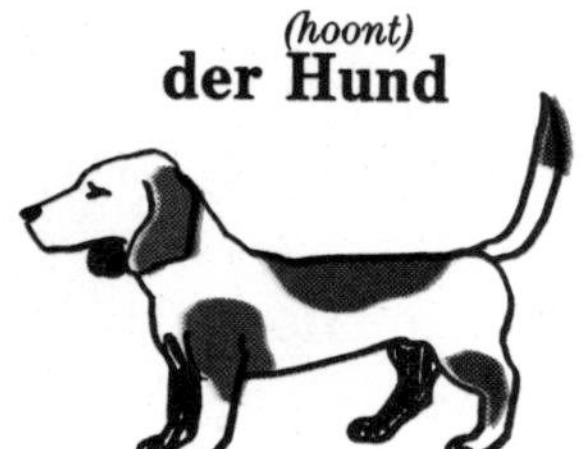

das Auto/der Wagen ______________ ______________

- ☐ **der Bäcker** *(beck-air)* . . . . the baker ______________
- ☐ **die Bäckerei** *(beck-air-eye)* . . . . the bakery ______________
- ☐ **der Ball** *(bahl)* . . . . the ball ______________
- ☐ **das Ballett** *(bah-let)* . . . . the ballet ______________
- ☐ **die Banane** *(ba-nah-nah)* . . . . the banana ______________

(kaht-tsa)
die Katze

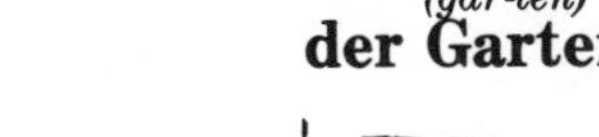

(gar-ten)
der Garten

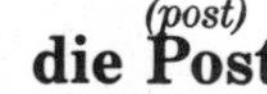

(post)
die Post

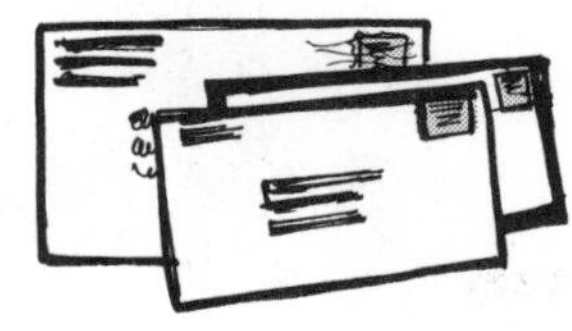

_______________ _______________ die Post

(breef-kah-sten)
der Briefkasten
mail box

(bloo-men)
die Blumen
flowers

(kling-el)
die Klingel
door bell

_______________ _______________ _______________

Peel off the next set of labels *(oont)* **und** wander through your *(house)* **Haus** learning these new *(vur-tair)* **Wörter.** Granted, it will be somewhat difficult to label your *(hoont)* **Hund, Katze,** *(oh-dair)* **oder die** *(bloo-men)* **Blumen,** but use your imagination.

Again, practice by asking yourself, *(voh)* **„Wo ist der** *(dair)* *(gar-ten)* **Garten?"** and reply, **„Dort ist der Garten."**

Now for the following:

Wo ist...

- ☐ **die Bank** *(bahnk)*.................... the bank _______________
- ☐ **das Beefsteak** *(beef-steak)*.............. the steak _______________
- ☐ **das Bett** *(bet)*...................... the bed _______________
- ☐ **besser** *(bess-air)*.................... better _______________
- ☐ **das Bier** *(beer)*..................... beer _______________

Step 4

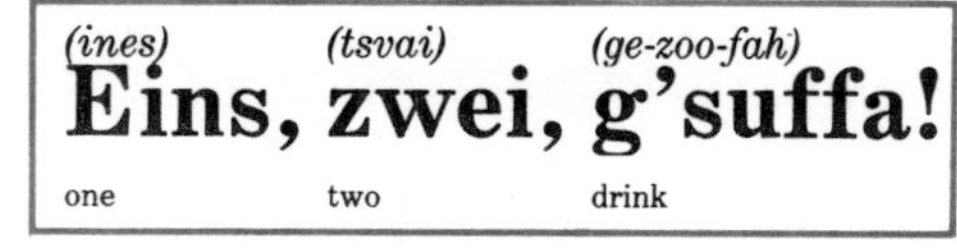

„In München steht ein Hofbräuhaus, Eins, zwei, g'suffa!"
(mewn-shen) (sh-tayt) (ine) (hohf-broy-house)
In Munich stands a brewery one two drink

When one thinks of **deutsche** *(doy-chah)* **Bier** *(beer)*-drinking songs, this **ist** one of the most famous. The **Hofbräuhaus** *(hohf-broy-house)* **ist** still to be found **in München** *(mewn-shen)* **und ist** an experience to visit. Let's learn how to join in on the refrain of **„Eins, zwei, g'suffa!"** *(ines) (tsvai) (ge-zoo-fah)* This **ist** where you are given a chance to swing your **Bier** stein once to the left **(eins)**, once to the right **(zwei)**, und then **es ist** time to take a drink **(g'suffa)**: **Eins, zwei, g'suffa!** When learning the following **Nummern** *(noo-mairn)* (numbers), notice the similarities (underlined) between **vier** *(fear)* (4) **und vierzehn** *(fear-tsayn)* (14), **fünf** *(fewnf)* (5) **und fünfzehn** *(fewnf-tsayn)* (15) **und** so on. After practicing **die Wörter** *(vur-tair)* out loud, cover the **Deutsch** *(doych)* **und** write out **die Nummern** 1 through 10 in the blanks.

0	*(nool)* **null**		
1	*(ines)* **eins**	11	*(elf)* **elf**
2	*(tsvai)* **zwei**	12	*(ts-vurlf)* **zwölf**
3	*(dry)* **drei**	13	*(dry-tsayn)* **dreizehn**
4	*(fear)* **vier**	14	*(fear-tsayn)* **vierzehn**
5	*(fewnf)* **fünf**	15	*(fewnf-tsayn)* **fünfzehn**
6	*(zex)* **sechs**	16	*(zex-tsayn)* **sechzehn**
7	*(zee-ben)* **sieben**	17	*(zeep-tsayn)* **siebzehn**
8	*(ahkt)* **acht**	18	*(ahkt-tsayn)* **achtzehn**
9	*(noyn)* **neun**	19	*(noyn-tsayn)* **neunzehn**
10	*(tsayn)* **zehn**	20	*(tsvahn-tsig)* **zwanzig**

0 null
1 ______________________
2 ______________________
3 ______________________
4 ______________________
5 ______________________
6 ______________________
7 ______________________
8 ______________________
9 ______________________
10 ______________________

- ☐ **blau** *(blau)* .... blue ______________
- ☐ **das Boot** *((boht)*.......................... the boat ______________
- ☐ **braun** *(brown)* .... brown ______________
- ☐ **bringen** *(bring-in)* .... to bring ______________
- ☐ **die Butter** *(boo-tair)*.................... the butter ______________

Use these **Nummern** *(noo-mairn)* on a daily basis. Count to yourself **auf** *(owf)* in **Deutsch** *(doych)* German when you brush your teeth, exercise, **oder** *(oh-dair)* commute to work. Now fill in the following blanks according to the **Nummern** *(noo-mairn)* given in parentheses.

Note: This is a good time to start learning these **zwei** *(tsvai)* important phrases.

(eehk) (murk-tah) **Ich möchte**	=	I would like	______________
(vir) (murk-ten) **wir möchten**	=	we would like	______________

(eehk) **Ich möchte** ______ (15) *(shtewk) (pah-peer)* **Stück Papier.** pieces of paper — *(vee-feel)* **Wieviel?** ______ (15)

Ich möchte ______ (10) *(post-kar-ten)* **Postkarten.** postcards — **Wieviel?** ______ (10)

Ich möchte ______ (11) *(breef-mar-ken)* **Briefmarken.** stamps — **Wieviel?** ______ (11)

Ich möchte ______ (8) *(lee-tair) (ben-tseen)* **Liter Benzin.** liters of gas — **Wieviel?** acht (8)

Ich möchte ______ (1) *(glahs) (oh-rahn-zhen-zahft)* **Glas Orangensaft.** glass of orange juice — **Wieviel?** ______ (1)

(vir) **Wir möchten** ______ (3) *(tah-sen) (tay)* **Tassen Tee.** cups of tea — **Wieviel?** ______ (3)

Wir möchten vier (4) *(tay-ah-tair-kar-ten)* **Theaterkarten.** theater tickets — **Wieviel?** ______ (4)

Wir möchten ______ (2) *(beer)* **Bier.** beer — **Wieviel?** ______ (2)

(eehk) **Ich möchte** ______ (12) *(frish-ah) (eye-air)* **frische Eier.** fresh eggs — **Wieviel?** ______ (12)

(vir) **Wir möchten** ______ (6) *(foont) (flaisch)* **Pfund Fleisch.** pounds of meat — **Wieviel?** ______ (6)

Wir möchten ______ (5) *(vah-sair)* **Glas Wasser.** glasses of water — **Wieviel?** ______ (5)

(eehk) **Ich möchte** ______ (7) *(vine)* **Glas Wein.** glasses of wine — **Wieviel?** ______ (7)

(vir) **Wir möchten** ______ (9) *(foont) (boo-tair)* **Pfund Butter.** pounds of butter — **Wieviel?** ______ (9)

Deutsch itself actually has no "C's," so you will note that all of these free **Wörter** are taken into **Deutsch** from other languages.

- ☐ **das Cafe** *(kah-fay)*.................. cafe ______________
- ☐ **der Champagner** *(shahm-pan-yair)*..... champagne ______________
- ☐ **die Chemie** *(shay-mee)*.............. chemistry ______________

Now see if you can translate the following thoughts into (doych) **Deutsch.** The answers are at the bottom of the (zigh-tah) **Seite** (page).

1. I would like 7 postcards.  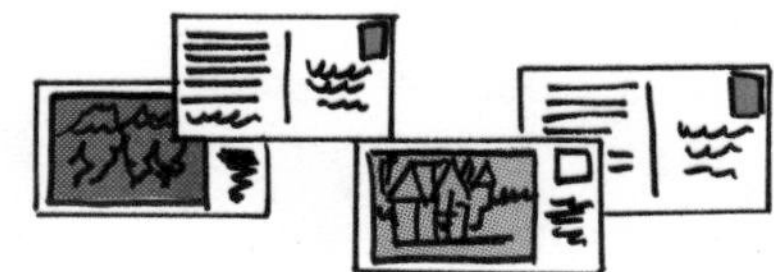

   ____

2. I would like 1 beer.  *Ich möchte ein Bier.*

3. We would like 2 glasses of water. 

   ____

4. We would like 3 theater tickets. 

   ____

Review **die** (noo-mairn) **Nummern** 1 through 20 (oont) **und** answer the following questions aloud, **und** then write the (ahnt-vor-ten) **Antworten** (answers) in the blank spaces.

(vee-feel) **Wieviel** (tish-ah) **Tische** (zint) **sind** (are) (here) **hier?**  ______________

Wieviel (lahm-pen) **Lampen sind hier?**  ______________

Wieviel (shtewl-ah) **Stühle sind hier?**  ______________

ANTWORTEN

1. **Ich möchte sieben Postkarten.**
2. **Ich möchte ein Bier.**
3. **Wir möchten zwei Glas Wasser.**
4. **Wir möchten drei Theaterkarten.**

Wieviel Uhren (uhr-en) sind (zint) hier?  ____________

Wieviel Fenster (fen-stair) sind hier? ____________

Wieviel Personen (pair-zoh-nen) sind hier?    sechs

Wieviel Männer (men-air) sind hier? ____________

Wieviel Frauen (frow-en) sind hier? ____________

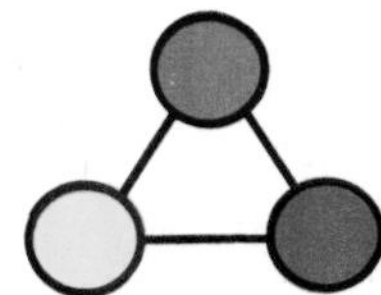

die (dee) Farben (fahr-ben)

colors

Step 5

Colors **sind** (zint) [are] the same **in Deutschland** (doych-lahnt) as **in Amerika** (ah-mair-ih-kah) — they just have different **Namen** (nah-men) [names]. You can easily recognize **violett** (vee-oh-let) as violet **oder purpur** (pur-pur) as purple. So when you are invited to someone's **Haus** (house) **und** you want to bring flowers, you will be able to order the correct color of flowers. (Contrary to American custom, **in Europa** (oy-roh-pah) [Europe] **rote** (roh-tah) **Blumen** (bloo-men) [flowers], **und** particularly **rote Rosen** (roh-zen) [roses], are only exchanged between lovers!) Let's learn the basic **Farben** (fahr-ben). Once you have read through **die** (dee) [the] **Liste** (lis-tah) [list] on the next **Seite** (zigh-tah), cover the **Deutsch** (doych) **mit** [with] your **Hand** (hahnt), **und** practice writing out the **Deutsch** next to the **Englisch** (eng-leash). Notice the similarities (underlined) between the **deutsche** (doy-chah) **und** the **englische** (eng-leash-ah) [English] **Wörter**.

☐ **das Chile** *(she-lay)*.................. Chile ____________
☐ **das China** *(she-nah)*.................. China ____________
☐ **chinesisch** *(shi-nay-zish)* .... Chinese ____________
☐ **der Chor** *(core)*...................... the choir ____________
☐ **christlich** *(krist-leeh)* .... christian ____________

weiß *(vice)* = white ______________________ **Das Boot** *(boht)* **ist weiß.**

schwarz *(shvarts)* = black ______________________ **Der Ball** *(bahl)* **ist schwarz.**

gelb *(gelp)* = yellow ______________________ **Die Banane** *(bah-nah-nah)* **ist gelb.**

rot *(roht)* = red ______________________ **Das Buch** *(boohk)* **ist rot.**

blau *(blau)* = blue ___blau___ **Das Auto** *(ow-toh)* **ist blau.**

grau *(grau)* = gray ______________________ **Der Elefant** *(ay-lay-fahnt)* **ist grau.**

braun *(brown)* = brown ______________________ **Der Stuhl** *(shtool)* **ist braun.**

grün *(grewn)* = green ______________________ **Das Gras** *(grahs)* **ist grün.**

rosa *(roh-zah)* = pink ______________________ **Die Blume** *(bloo-mah)* **ist rosa.**

bunt *(boont)* = multi-colored ______________________ **Die Lampe** *(lahm-pah)* **ist bunt.**

Now peel off the next **zehn** *(tsayn)* labels **und** *(oont)* proceed to label these **Farben in** your **Haus.**

Now let's practice using these **Wörter.**

Wo *(voh)* **ist das weiße** *(vice-ah)* **Boot** *(boht)***?** — **Dort ist das** ___weiße___ **Boot.**

Wo ist der graue *(grau-ah)* **Tisch** *(tish)***?** — **Dort ist der** _______ **Tisch.**

Wo ist der braune *(brown-ah)* **Stuhl** *(shtool)***?** — **Dort ist der** _______ **Stuhl.**

Wo ist der weiße *(vice-ah)* **Ball** *(bahl)***?** — **Dort ist der** _______ **Ball.**

Wo ist die bunte *(boon-tah)* **Lampe** *(lahm-pah)***?** — **Dort ist die** _______ **Lampe.**

Wo ist das rote *(roh-tah)* **Buch** *(boohk)***?** — **Dort ist das** _______ **Buch.**

- ☐ **der Dezember** *(day-tsem-bair)*......... December ______________
- ☐ **der Doktor** *(dohk-tor)*............... the doctor ______________
  — The doctor is a title; **der Arzt ist** the word for a medical doctor. ______________
- ☐ **die Drogerie** *(droh-gih-ree)*........... the drugstore ______________

Wo ist die *(grewn-ah)* grüne *(tewr)* Tür? Dort ist die _______ Tür.

Wo ist das *(roh-zah)* rosa *(house)* Haus? Dort ist das _______ Haus.

Wo ist die *(gel-bah)* gelbe *(bah-nah-nah)* Banane? Dort ist die _______ Banane.

Note: *(owf)* **Auf** (In) *(doych)* **Deutsch** (German) the verb for "to have" **ist „***(hah-ben)* **haben."**

(eehk) **ich** *(hah-bah)* **habe** = I have _______________ *(vir)* **wir haben** = we have _______________

Let's review *(murk-ten)* **möchten und** learn *(hah-ben)* **haben**. Be sure to repeat each sentence out loud.

(eehk) **Ich** *(murk-tah)* **möchte ein** *(glahs)* **Glas Bier.**	**Ich** *(hah-bah)* **habe ein Glas Bier.**
(vir) **Wir möchten** *(tsvai)* **zwei Glas** *(vine)* **Wein.**	**Wir** *(hah-ben)* **haben zwei Glas Wein.**
Ich möchte ein Glas *(vah-sair)* **Wasser.**	**Wir haben ein Haus.**
Wir möchten einen *(zah-laht)* **Salat.**	**Ich habe ein Haus in** *(ah-mair-ih-kah)* **Amerika.**
Wir möchten ein *(ow-toe)* **Auto.**	**Ich habe ein Auto.**
Wir möchten ein Auto in *(oy-roh-pah)* **Europa.**	**Wir haben ein Auto in Europa.**

Now fill in the following blanks **mit** the correct form of **„haben" oder „möchten."**

Wir haben _______________ *(dry)* **drei** *(ow-toes)* **Autos.**
(we have)

_______________ *(tsvai)* **zwei Theaterkarten.**
(we would like)

_______________ **ein** *(bilt)* **Bild.**
(I have)

_______________ *(zee-ben)* **sieben Postkarten.**
(I would like)

- ☐ **das Eis** *(ice)*. . . . . ice cream _______________
- ☐ **der Elefant** *(ay-lay-fahnt)*. . . . . the elephant _______________
- ☐ **das England** *(eng-lahnt)*. . . . . England _______________
  — where they speak **Englisch** _______________
- ☐ **das Europa** *(oy-roh-pah)*. . . . . Europe _______________

(here) **Hier ist** a quick review of the *(fahr-ben)* **Farben.** Draw lines between **die** *(doych-en)* **deutschen Wörter** *(oont)* **und die** *(reehk-tee-gah)* **richtige** (correct) **Farbe.** On your mark, get set, *GO!*

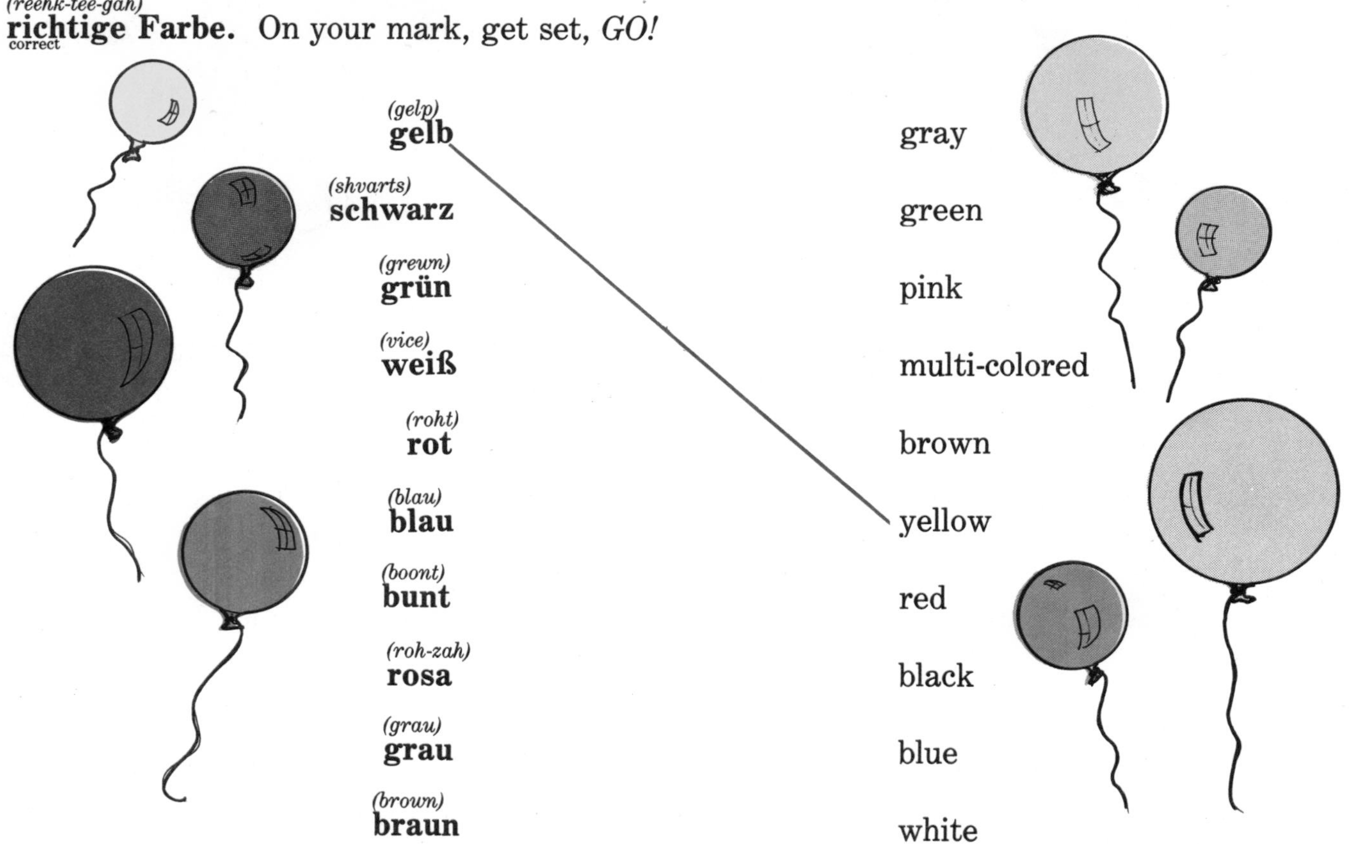

(noon) **Nun,** take a deep breath. Test your pronunciation on these *(doy-chah)* **deutsche** (German) proverbs.

(bore-gen) **Borgen** (borrowing) *(brinkt)* **bringt** (brings) *(zore-gen)* **Sorgen.** (sorrows)

(vee) **Wie** *(guh-vohn-en)* **gewonnen,** *(zoh)(tsair-rohn-en)* **so zerronnen!** (easy come, easy go)

(noon) **Nun,** (now) try these **deutsche** tongue-twisters. Are you ready?

(kly-nah) **Kleine** (small) *(kin-dair)* **Kinder** (children) *(kur-nen)* **können** *(kai-nah)* **keine** (can't) *(kirsh-kair-nah)* **Kirschkerne** *(knah-ken)* **knacken.** (crack cherry stones)

(kai-zairz) **Kaisers** (the Kaiser's) *(kurk-hen)* **Köchin** (cook) *(kahn)* **kann** *(kai-nen)* **keinen** (can't) *(kalps-kopf)* **Kalbskopf** *(kohk-hen)* **kochen.** (cook calf's head)

Don't worry if this seems difficult at first. Continue with the next Steps and come back to it later. You'll be surprised how quickly you improve — especially with practice!

- ☐ **europäisch** *(oy-roh-pay-ish)* . . . . European ____________
- ☐ **die Familie** *(fah-mee-lee-yah)* . . . . the family ____________
- ☐ **fantastisch** *(fahn-tahs-tish)* . . . . fantastic ____________
  — ex. **Das ist fantastisch!**
- ☐ **der Februar** *(fay-broo-ahr)* . . . . February ____________

Step 6

Before starting this Step, go back **und** review Step 4. Make sure you can count to *(tsvahn-tsig)* **zwanzig** without looking back at **das** *(boohk)* **Buch**. Let's learn the larger *(noo-mairn)* **Nummern** now, so if something costs more than 20 *(day-em)* **DM** you will know exactly *(vee-feel)* **wieviel** it costs. After practicing aloud *(dee)* **die deutschen Nummern** 10 through 100 below, write these *(noo-mairn)* **Nummern** in the blanks provided. Again, notice the similarities between numbers such as *(fewnf-tsig)* **fünfzig** (50), *(fewnf)* **fünf** (5) **und** *(feunf-tsayn)* **fünfzehn** (15).

10	*(tsayn)* **zehn**	**(vier + sechs = zehn)**
20	*(tsvahn-tsig)* **zwanzig**	*(tsvai)* **(zwei = 2)**
30	*(dry-tsig)* **dreißig**	**(drei = 3)**
40	*(fear-tsig)* **vierzig**	**(vier = 4)**
50	*(fewnf-tsig)* **fünfzig**	**(fünf = 5)**
60	*(zex-tsig)* **sechzig**	**(sechs = 6)**
70	*(zeep-tsig)* **siebzig**	*(zee-ben)* **(sieben = 7)**
80	*(ahkt-tsig)* **achtzig**	**(acht = 8)**
90	*(noyn-tsig)* **neunzig**	**(neun = 9)**
100	*(hoon-dairt)* **hundert**	
1000	*(tau-zent)* **tausend**	

10 zehn

20 __________

30 __________

40 __________

50 __________

60 __________

70 __________

80 __________

90 __________

100 __________

1000 __________

Now take a logical guess. *(vee)* **Wie** would you write (**und** say) the following? The answers *(zint)* **sind** at the bottom of the *(zigh-tah)* **Seite.**

400 __________ 600 __________

2000 __________ 5300 __________

ANTWORTEN

400 = vierhundert
2000 = zweitausend
600 = sechshundert
5300 = fünftausenddreihundert

The unit of currency **in** *(doych-lahnt)* **Deutschland ist die Deutsche Mark**, abbreviated *(day-em)* **DM.** Currency **ist** called *(shy-nah)* **Scheine und** coins are called *(kline-gelt)* **Kleingeld.** Just as **ein** *(ah-mair-ih-kahn-ish-air)* **amerikanischer** *(doh-lar)* **Dollar** can be broken down into 100 pennies, *(ine-ah)* **eine deutsche Mark** can be broken down into 100 *(fen-ee-gah)* **Pfennige.** A coin is called **ein** *(gelt-shtewk)* **Geldstück** (money piece) **und** you will also hear *(shy-nah)* **Scheine** (currency) referred to as *(gelt-shy-nah)* **Geldscheine.** Let's learn the various kinds of *(shy-nah)* **Scheine** (currency) **und** *(kline-gelt)* **Kleingeld** (coins). Always be sure to practice each **Wort** out loud. You might want to exchange some money *(noon)* **nun** (now) so that you can familiarize yourself **mit** the various *(kline-gelt)* **Kleingeld** (or *(gelt-shtewk-en)* **Geldstücken) und Scheine** (or *(gelt-shy-nen)* **Geldscheinen**).

(ine) **ein** (a) *(fewnf-mark-shine)* **Fünfmarkschein** (5-mark bill)

(ine) **ein** (a) *(ine-fen-ig-shtewk)* **Einpfennigstück** (1-pfennig coin)

ein (a) *(tsayn-mark-shine)* **Zehnmarkschein** (10-mark bill)

ein (a) *(tsvai-fen-ig-shtewk)* **Zweipfennigstück** (2-pfennig coin)

ein Zwanzigmarkschein

ein (a) *(fewnf-fen-ig-shtewk)* **Fünfpfennigstück** (5-pfennig coin)

ein Fünfzigmarkschein

ein *(tsayn-fen-ig-shtewk)* **Zehnpfennigstück**

ein Hundertmarkschein

ein *(fewnf-tsig-fen-ig-shtewk)* **Fünfzigpfennigstück**

ein Fünfhundertmarkschein

ein Markstück

ein Tausendmarkschein

ein *(tsvai-mark-shtewk)* **Zweimarkstück**

ein *(fewnf-mark-shtewk)* **Fünfmarkstück**

- ☐ **der Film** *(film)* . . . . film ____________
- ☐ **finden** *(fin-den)* . . . . to find ____________
  — ex. **Ich finde das Hotelzimmer.** ____________
- ☐ **der Finger** *(fing-air)* . . . . finger ____________
- ☐ **der Fisch** *(fish)* . . . . fish ____________

Review **die Nummern** *(tsayn)* **zehn** through *(tau-zent)* **tausend** again. *(noon)* **Nun,** how do you say "twenty-two" *(oh-dair)* **oder** "fifty-three" *(owf)* **auf** (in) **Deutsch?** (German) You basically talk backwards—*(zwei-und-zwanzig)* "two and twenty" **oder** *(drei-und-fünfzig)* "three and fifty." See if you can say **und** write out **die Nummern** on this *(zigh-tah)* **Seite.**

The answers *(zint)* **sind** at the bottom of the **Seite.**

a. 25 =	______ (5 + 20)	b. 36 =	______ (6 + 30)
c. 47 =	siebenundvierzig (7 + 40)	d. 93 =	______ (3 + 90)
e. 84 =	______ (4 + 80)	f. 68 =	______ (8 + 60)
g. 51 =	______ (1 + 50)	h. 72 =	______ (2 + 70)

To ask how much something costs *(owf)* **auf Deutsch,** one asks, *(vee-feel) (koh-stet) (dahs)* **„Wieviel kostet das?"** *(noon)* **Nun** (now) answer the following questions based on the *(noo-mairn)* **Nummern** (numbers) in parentheses.

1. *(vee-feel) (koh-stet)* **Wieviel kostet das?** (How much costs that?) **Es kostet** zehn (10) **Mark.**
2. **Wieviel kostet das?** **Es kostet** ______ (20) **Mark.**
3. **Wieviel kostet das Buch?** **Es kostet** ______ (17) **Mark.**
4. **Wieviel kostet das** *(ow-toh)* **Auto?** **Es kostet** ______ (2000) **Mark.**
5. **Wieviel kostet** *(dair)* **der Film?** **Es kostet** ______ (5) **Mark.**
6. **Wieviel kostet das** *(tsi-mair)* **Zimmer?** **Es kostet** ______ (24) **Mark.**
7. **Wieviel kostet das** *(bilt)* **Bild?** **Es kostet** ______ (923) **Mark.**

ANTWORTEN

a. **fünfundzwanzig**	f. **achtundsechzig**	3. **siebzehn**
b. **sechsunddreißig**	g. **einundfünfzig**	4. **zweitausend**
c. **siebenundvierzig**	h. **zweiundsiebzig**	5. **fünf**
d. **dreiundneunzig**	1. **zehn**	6. **vierundzwanzig**
e. **vierundachtzig**	2. **zwanzig**	7. **neunhundertdreiundzwanzig**

Congratulations!

Step 7

Heute, morgen, und gestern

(hoy-tah) **Heute** (today), (more-gen) **morgen** (tomorrow), (oont) **und** (and) (ges-tairn) **gestern** (yesterday)

(kah-len-dair) der Kalender						
Eine (voh-kah) **Woche** (week) (haht) **hat sieben** (tah-gah) **Tage** (days).						
(zohn-tahk) **Sonntag**	(mohn-tahk) **Montag**	(deens-tahk) **Dienstag**	(mit-vohk) **Mittwoch**	(doh-nairs-tahk) **Donnerstag**	(fry-tahk) **Freitag**	(zahms-tahk) **Samstag**
1	2	3	4	5	6	7

Es ist (zair) **sehr** (very) important to know the days of the week **und** the various parts of the (tahk) **Tag** (day). Let's learn them. Be sure to say them aloud before filling in the blanks below.

(zohn-tahk) **Sonntag** ____________	(mohn-tahk) **Montag** *Montag*
(deens-tahk) **Dienstag** ____________	(mit-vohk) **Mittwoch** ____________
(doh-nairs-tahk) **Donnerstag** ____________	(fry-tahk) **Freitag** ____________
(zahms-tahk) **Samstag** ____________	

If (hoy-tah) **heute ist Mittwoch**, then (more-gen) **morgen ist Donnerstag und** (ges-tairn) **gestern** (vahr) **war** (was) **Dienstag.** (noon) **Nun,** you supply the correct answers. If **heute ist Montag**, then **morgen ist** ____________ **und gestern war** ____________. Or, if **heute ist Montag**, then *morgen* **ist Dienstag und** ____________ **war Sonntag. Was ist heute? Heute ist** ____________.

(noon) **Nun,** peel off the next (zee-ben) **sieben** labels (oont) **und** put them on a (kah-len-dair) **Kalender** you use every (tahk) **Tag** (day).

From **nun** on—Monday **ist „Montag!"**

- ☐ **frei** *(fry)* .... free, no charge, available ____________
- ☐ **der Garten** *(gar-ten)* .... garden ____________
- ☐ **das Glas** *(glahs)* .... glass ____________
- ☐ **gut** *(goot)* .... good ____________
  — ex. **nicht gut** = not good ____________

There are **vier** *(fear)* parts to each **Tag.** *(tahk)* day

morning = **der Morgen** *(more-gen)*	der Morgen
afternoon = **der Nachmittag** *(nahk-mit-tahk)*	
evening = **der Abend** *(ah-bent)*	
night = **die Nacht** *(nahkt)*	

Notice that **morgen** means "tomorrow" **und der Morgen** means "morning" **auf Deutsch.**

Nun, fill in the following blanks **und** then check your **Antworten** *(ahnt-vor-ten)* at the bottom of the **Seite.** *(zigh-táh)* page

a. Sunday morning = Sonntag morgen
b. Friday evening = ____
c. Saturday evening = ____
d. Monday morning = ____
e. Wednesday morning = ____
f. Tuesday afternoon = ____
g. Thursday afternoon = ____
h. Thursday night = ____
i. yesterday evening = ____
j. this afternoon (today) = heute nachmittag
k. this morning = ____
l. tomorrow afternoon = ____
m. tomorrow evening = ____

ANTWORTEN

a. **Sonntag morgen**
b. **Freitag abend**
c. **Samstag abend**
d. **Montag morgen**
e. **Mittwoch morgen**
f. **Dienstag nachmittag**
g. **Donnerstag nachmittag**
h. **Donnerstag nacht**
i. **gestern abend**
j. **heute nachmittag**
k. **heute morgen**
l. **morgen nachmittag**
m. **morgen abend**

So **mit** [with] merely **elf** *(vur-tair)* **Wörter** you can specify any day of the *(voh-kah)* **Woche** [week] **und** any time of the *(tahk)* **Tag.** **Die Wörter** *(hoy-tah)* **heute,** *(more-gen)* **morgen, und** *(ges-tairn)* **gestern** will be *(zair)* **sehr** important for you in making reservations *(oont)* **und** appointments, in getting *(tay-ah-tair-kar-ten)* **Theaterkarten und** many things you will wish to do. Knowing the parts of the *(tahk)* **Tag** will help you to learn **und** understand the various *(doy-chah)* **deutsche** greetings below. Practice these every *(tahk)* **Tag nun** until your trip.

good morning	=	*(goo-ten) (more-gen)* **Guten Morgen**	______________
good day (hello)	=	*(goo-ten) (tahk)* **Guten Tag**	______________
good evening	=	*(goo-ten) (ah-bent)* **Guten Abend**	Guten Abend
good night	=	*(goo-tah) (nahkt)* **Gute Nacht**	______________
How are you?	=	*(vee) (gate) (ee-nen)* **Wie geht es Ihnen?**	______________

Take the next *(fear)* **vier** labels *(oont)* **und** stick them on the appropriate *(ding-ah)* **Dinge** [things] in your *(house)* **Haus.** *(vee)* **Wie** about the bathroom mirror *(fewr)* **für Guten Morgen?** *(oh-dair)* **Oder** the front door **für Guten Abend?** *(oh-dair)* **Oder** your alarm clock *(fewr)* **für** [for] **Gute Nacht? Oder** your kitchen cabinet **für Guten Tag?** Remember that, whenever you enter shops **und** stores **in** *(doych-lahnt)* **Deutschland,** you will hear the appropriate greeting for the time of day. Don't be surprised. **Es ist** a *(zair)* **sehr** [very] friendly custom. Everyone greets everyone *(oont)* **und** you should too, if you really want to enjoy *(doych-lahnt)* **Deutschland!** You *(zint)* **sind** about one-fourth of your way through **das** *(boohk)* **Buch und es ist** a good time to quickly review **die** *(vur-tair)* **Wörter** you *(hah-ben)* **haben** learned before doing the crossword puzzle on the next *(zigh-tah)* **Seite.** *(feel)* **Viel** *(shpahss)* **Spaß und** *(feel)* **viel** *(glewk)* **Glück!** *(oh-dair)* **Oder,** as we say *(owf)* **auf Englisch,** much fun and lots of luck!

ANTWORTEN TO CROSSWORD PUZZLE

ACROSS

1. Dienstag
2. Nachmittag
3. Mittwoch
4. heute
5. Donnerstag
6. fünf
7. Abend
8. dreißig
9. wieviel
10. Amerika
11. sieben
12. frei
13. Bank
14. gestern
15. Wein
16. blau
17. der/die/das
18. sechzig
19. rosa
20. haben
21. Tag
22. vier
23. gelb
24. zwanzig
25. gut
26. warum
27. Büro
28. Bier
29. in

DOWN

1. neun
2. Sonntag
3. Auto
4. Nacht
5. Familie
6. morgen
7. Montag
8. Samstag
9. weiß
10. wer
11. elf
12. Freitag
13. Bus
14. kommen
15. Mark
16. bunt
17. Bild
18. eins
19. rot
20. Tee
21. Bett
22. vierzig
23. grau
24. Zug
25. grün
26. wo
27. in
28. schwarz

(kroits-vort-rate-sel)
DAS KREUZWORTRÄTSEL

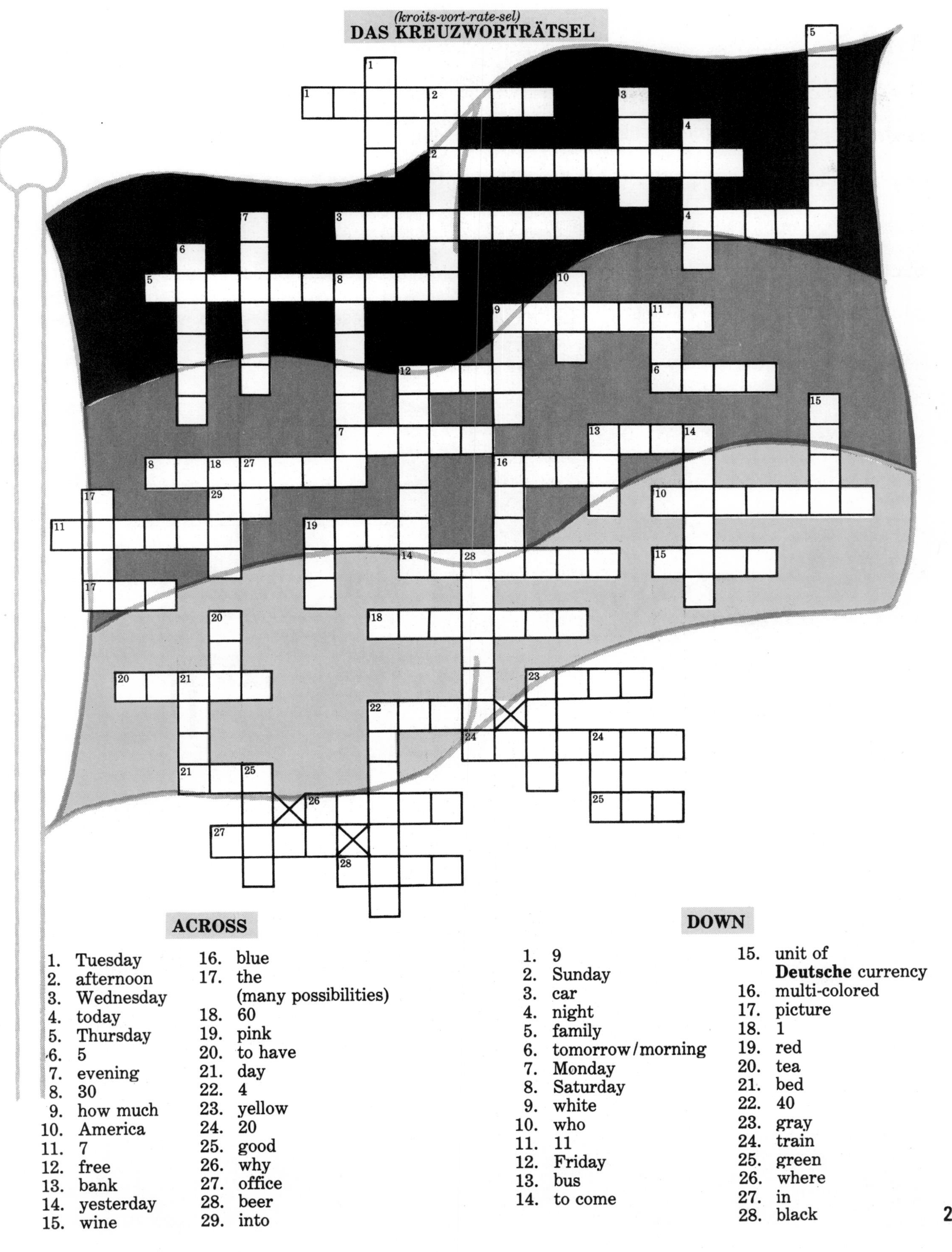

ACROSS

1. Tuesday
2. afternoon
3. Wednesday
4. today
5. Thursday
6. 5
7. evening
8. 30
9. how much
10. America
11. 7
12. free
13. bank
14. yesterday
15. wine
16. blue
17. the (many possibilities)
18. 60
19. pink
20. to have
21. day
22. 4
23. yellow
24. 20
25. good
26. why
27. office
28. beer
29. into

DOWN

1. 9
2. Sunday
3. car
4. night
5. family
6. tomorrow/morning
7. Monday
8. Saturday
9. white
10. who
11. 11
12. Friday
13. bus
14. to come
15. unit of **Deutsche** currency
16. multi-colored
17. picture
18. 1
19. red
20. tea
21. bed
22. 40
23. gray
24. train
25. green
26. where
27. in
28. black

Step 8

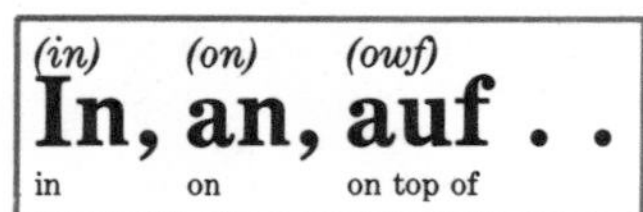

(doy-chah) **Deutsche** prepositions (words like "in," "on," "through," and "next to") *(zint)* **sind** easy to learn *(oont)* **und** they allow you to be precise **mit** a minimum of effort. Instead of having to point *(zex)* **sechs** times at a piece of yummy pastry you wish to order, you can explain precisely which one you want by saying **es ist** behind, in front of, next to, *(oh-dair)* **oder** under the piece of pastry which the salesperson **ist** starting to pick up. Let's learn some of these little *(vur-tair)* **Wörter** which are *(zair)* **sehr** similar to *(eng-leash)* **Englisch.** Study the examples below.

(ows) **aus** = out of / from

in = into / in

(nay-ben) **neben** = next to

(oon-tair) **unter** = under

(ew-bair) **über** = over

(dair) **Der** *(mahn)* **Mann** *(gate)* **geht** (goes) **in** das *(noy-ah)* **neue Hotel.**

(dee) **Die** *(frow)* **Frau** *(kohmt)* **kommt** (comes) *(ows)* **aus** *(daim)* **dem** *(goo-ten)* **guten Hotel.**

Der *(arts-t)* **Arzt** (doctor) **ist in** *(daim)* **dem guten Hotel.**

Das *(noy-ah)* **neue** *(bilt)* **Bild ist über** *(daim)* **dem Tisch.**

Das neue Bild ist neben der Uhr.

Der braune Tisch ist unter dem Bild.

Der *(grau-ah)* **graue** *(hoont)* **Hund ist neben dem Tisch.**

Die *(grewn-ah)* **grüne Uhr ist über dem Tisch.**

Die grüne Uhr ist neben dem Bild.

- ☐ **ich** *(eehk)*. I
- ☐ **die Information** *(in-for-mah-tsee-ohn)*. . . information
  — also known as **Auskunft**
- ☐ **interessant** *(in-tair-es-sahnt)*. . . . . interesting
  — ex. **Das ist sehr interessant.**

Fill in the blanks below **mit** the correct prepositions according to the *(bil-dair)* **Bilder** (pictures) on the previous *(zigh-tah)* **Seite.**

Der *(mahn)* **Mann** *(gate)* **geht** in **das neue Hotel.**

Der *(grau-ah)* **graue Hund ist** ________ **dem Tisch.**

Die grüne Uhr ist ________ *(daim)* **dem Tisch.**

Der *(arts-t)* **Arzt ist** ________ *(daim)* **dem guten Hotel.**

Die *(grewn-ah)* **grüne Uhr ist** ________ **dem Bild.**

Das *(noy-ah)* **neue Bild ist** ________ **dem Tisch.**

Der braune Tisch ist ________ **dem Bild.**

Das neue Bild ist ________ **der Uhr.**

Die *(frow)* **Frau kommt** ______ **dem guten Hotel.**

(noon) **Nun,** answer these questions based on the *(bil-dair)* **Bilder** on the previous *(zigh-tah)* **Seite.**

(voh) **Wo ist der** *(arts-t)* **Arzt?** ________________________________

Wo ist der *(hoont)* **Hund?** ________________________________

Wo ist der Tisch? ________________________________

Wo ist das Bild? ________________________________

(vahs) **Was** *(mahkt)* **macht** (does) *(dee)* **die Frau?** ________________________________

Was *(mahkt)* **macht** (does) **der Mann?** ________________________________

Ist die Uhr *(grewn)* **grün?** Ja, die Uhr ist grün.

Ist der Hund *(grau)* **grau?** Ja,

- ☐ **das Institut** *(in-stee-toot)*.............. institution ____________
- ☐ **das Italien** *(ee-tah-lee-en)*.............. Italy ____________
  —where they speak **Italienisch** *(ee-tah-lee-ay-nish)* ____________
- ☐ **ja** *(yah)*.............................. yes ____________
- ☐ **die Jacke** *(yah-kah)*.................. jacket ____________

Nun *(noon)* for some more practice **mit deutschen** prepositions!

auf *(owf)* = on top of (horizontal surfaces)

an *(on)* = on/upon (vertical surfaces)

vor *(for)* = in front of

hinter *(hin-tair)* = behind

Das *(dahs)* **Glas Wasser** *(vah-sair)* **ist auf** *(owf)* **dem** *(daim)* **Tisch.**	**Das Glas Wasser ist ______ dem Tisch.**
Das bunte *(boon-tah)* **Bild ist an** *(on)* **der Wand** *(vahnt)*.	**Das bunte Bild ist** ___an___ **der Wand.**
Die gelbe *(gel-bah)* **Lampe ist hinter** *(hin-tair)* **dem Tisch.**	**Die gelbe Lampe ist ______ dem Tisch.**
Der braune Tisch ist vor *(for)* **dem Bett.**	**Der braune Tisch ist ______ dem Bett.**
Das bunte *(boon-tah)* **Bett ist hinter dem braunen Tisch.**	**Das bunte Bett ist ____________ dem braunen Tisch.**

Answer the following **Fragen** *(frah-gen)*, questions, based on the **Bilder** *(bil-dair)*, by filling in the blanks **mit** the correct prepositions. Choose the prepositions from those you **haben** *(hah-ben)* just learned.

Wo *(voh)* **ist das rote** *(roh-tah)* **Buch** *(boohk)*? — **Das rote Buch** *(boohk)* **ist ______ dem braunen Tisch.**

Wo ist der blaue Bus *(boos)*? — **Der blaue Bus ist ______ dem grauen Hotel.**

- ☐ **das Jahr** *(yahr)* .... year ____________
- ☐ **der Januar** *(yah-noo-ar)* .... January ____________
- ☐ **das Japan** *(ya-pahn)* .... Japan ____________
  — where they speak **Japanisch** *(ya-pahn-ish)*
- ☐ **das Journal** *(zhur-nahl)* .... magazine ____________

Wo *(voh)* **ist das graue Telefon?** *(tay-lay-fohn)* **Wo ist der grüne Teppich?** *(grewn-ah) (tep-eeh)* **Wo ist das Bild?**

Das *(dahs)* **graue Telefon ist** ______________ **der weißen Wand.** *(vice-en) (vahnt)*

Das graue Telefon ist ______________ **dem bunten Bild.** *(daim) (boon-ten)*

Das graue Telefon ist __________ **dem schwarzen Tisch.** *(shvar-tsen)*

Der grüne Teppich ist __________ **dem schwarzen Tisch.**

Das Bild ist ___an___ **der weißen Wand.** *(vice-en) (vahnt)*

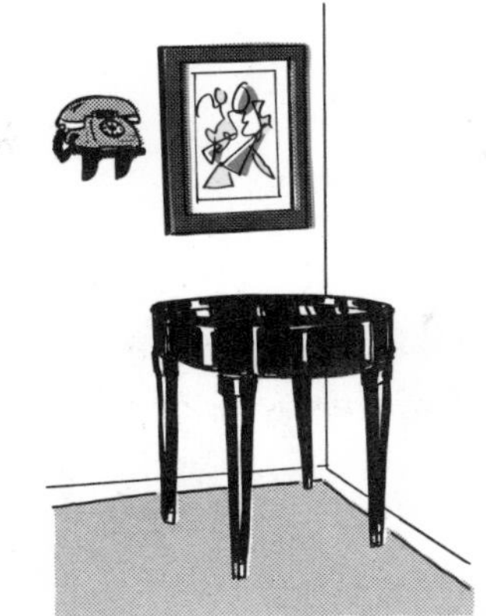

Nun fill in each blank on the **Hotel** below **mit** the best possible preposition. The correct **Antworten sind** *(ahnt-vor-ten)* at the bottom of the **Seite. Viel** *(feel)* **Spaß.**

1. ______________
2. ______________
3. ______________
4. ______________
5. ______________
6. ___in___
7. ______________
8. ______________
9. ______________
10. ______________

HOTEL RITTER

ANTWORTEN

1. **über**	3. **hinter**	5. **in**	7. **neben**	9. **unter**
2. **auf**	4. **an**	6. **in**	8. **vor**	10. **aus**

Step 9

(jah-noo-ar) Januar, (fay-broo-ar) Februar, (merts) März

Dreißig Tage (haht) hat (has) (zep-tem-bair) September, (ah-pril) April, (you-nee) Juni, und (noh-vem-bair) November . . .

Sound familiar? You (hah-ben) **haben** learned the days of the (voh-kah) **Woche**, so now **es ist** time to learn **die** (moh-nah-tah) **Monate** (months) of the (yahr) **Jahr** (year) **und** all the different kinds of (vet-tair) **Wetter** (weather) which you might encounter on your holiday. For example, you ask about **das** (vet-tair) **Wetter auf Deutsch** just as you would **auf Englisch**—**„(vee) Wie (how) ist (is) das (the) Wetter (weather) (hoy-tah) heute? (today)"** Practice all the possible answers to this (frah-gah) **Frage** (question) **und** (don) **dann** (then) write the following answers in the blanks below.

(vee) Wie ist das Wetter (hoy-tah) heute?

Es (rayg-net) regnet (rains) heute. ______________________________

Es (shnait) schneit (snows) heute. ______________________________

Es ist (varm) warm (warm) heute. ______________________________

Es ist (kahlt) kalt (cold) heute. Es ist kalt heute.

Es ist (shurn) schön (pretty) heute. ______________________________

Es ist (shleckt) schlecht (bad) heute. ______________________________

Es ist (hice) heiß (hot) heute. ______________________________

Es ist (nay-blig) neblig (foggy) heute. ______________________________

Nun practice the **Wörter** on the next **Seite** aloud **und** (don) **dann** (then) fill in the blanks **mit** the names of the month **und** the appropriate weather report.

- ☐ **der Juli** *(you-lee)*.................... July ______________
- ☐ **der Juni** *(you-nee)*.................... June ______________

— Mit den freien K Wörtern, notice how often **Englisch** "c" becomes "k" **auf Deutsch.**

- ☐ **der Kaffee** *(kah-fay)*.................. coffee ______________
- ☐ **das Kaffeehaus** *(kah-fay-house)*....... coffee house ______________

(im) (jah-noo-ar) **im Januar** _____ *in*	*(shnait)* **Es schneit im Januar.** _____
(fay-broo-ar) **im Februar** _____	*(owk)* **Es schneit auch im Februar.** _____ *also*
(merts) **im März** _____	*(rayg-net)* **Es regnet im März.** Es regnet im März.
(ah-pril) **im April** _____	**Es regnet auch im April.** _____
(my) **im Mai** _____	*(vin-dig)* **Es ist windig im Mai.** _____ *windy*
(you-nee) **im Juni** _____	**Es ist auch windig im Juni.** _____
(you-lee) **im Juli** im Juli	*(varm)* **Es ist warm im Juli.** _____
(ow-goost) **im August** _____	*(hice)* **Es ist heiß im August.** _____
(zep-tem-bair) **im September** _____	*(shurn)* **Es ist schön im September.** _____
(ohk-toh-bair) **im Oktober** _____	*(nay-blig)* **Es ist neblig im Oktober.** _____
(noh-vem-bair) **im November** _____	*(kahlt)* **Es ist kalt im November.** _____
(day-tsem-bair) **im Dezember** _____	*(shleckt)* **Es ist schlecht im Dezember.** _____

Nun answer the following *(frah-gen)* **Fragen** based on the *(bil-dair)* **Bilder** to the right.

Wie ist das *(vet-tair)* **Wetter im** *(in)* *(fay-broo-ar)* **Februar?** _____

Wie ist das Wetter im *(ah-pril)* **April?** _____

Wie ist das Wetter im *(my)* **Mai?** _____

Wie ist das Wetter im *(ow-goost)* **August?** _____

Ist das Wetter *(hoy-tah)* **heute** *(today)* **gut oder schlecht?** _____

☐ **der Kakao** *(ka-kow)*	hot chocolate	_____
☐ **kalt** *(kahlt)*	cold	_____
☐ **die Karotten** *(kah-roh-ten)*	carrots	_____
☐ **die Karten** *(kar-ten)*	cards	_____
☐ **kommen** *((koh-men)*	to come	_____

Nun **für** *(fewr)* the seasons of the **Jahr** *(yahr)* [year] . . .

der Winter *(vin-tair)*	der Sommer *(zoh-mair)*	der Herbst *(hairp-st)* [autumn]	der Frühling *(frew-ling)* [spring]

der Winter ____________ ____________ ____________

Es ist kalt *(kahlt)* **im** [in] **Winter.**	**Es ist heiß** *(hice)* **im Sommer.**	**Es ist windig** *(vin-dig)* **im Herbst.**	**Es regnet** *(rayg-net)* **im Frühling.**

At this point **es ist eine gute** *(goo-tah)* [good] **Idee** *(ee-day)* [idea] to familiarize yourself **mit europäischen** *(oy-roh-pay-ish-en)* [European] **Temperaturen** *(tem-pair-ah-toor-en)* [temperatures]. Carefully read the typical weather forecasts below **und** study the thermometer because temperatures **in Europa** *(oy-roh-pah)* are calculated on the basis of Centigrade (not Fahrenheit).

Fahrenheit *(fah-ren-hait)*	**Celsius** *(sell-see-oos)* [Centigrade]	
212° F ——	100° C	**Wasser** *(vah-sair)* **kocht** [boils]
98.6° F ——	37° C	**Normale** *(nor-mah-lah)* [normal] **Bluttemperatur** [blood temperature]
68° F ——	20° C	
32° F ——	0° C	**Süßwasser** *(zeus-vah-sair)* [fresh water] **friert** [freezes]
0° F ——	-17.8° C	**Salzwasser** *(zahlts-vah-sair)* [salt water] **friert** [freezes]
-10° F ——	-23.3° C	

Das Wetter *(vet-tair)* **für** *(fewr)* **Montag, den** *(dain)* **21. März** *(merts)*:

kalt und windig
Temperatur *(tem-pair-ah-toor)*: **5 Grad** *(graht)* [degrees]

Das Wetter für Dienstag, den 18. Juli:

warm und schön
Temperatur: 20 Grad

- ☐ **der Kilometer** *(kee-loh-may-tair)*....... kilometer ____________
  — A **Kilometer ist** 1000 meters. ____________
- ☐ **kochen** *(kohk-hen)*.................... to cook ____________
  — ex. **Ich koche in der Küche.** ____________
- ☐ **das Konzert** *(kohn-tsairt)*............. concert ____________

(kin-dair) Kinder, *(kew-sha)* Küche, und *(kirh-ha)* Kirche

children / kitchen / church

Step 10

Just as we have the "3 R's" *(owf)* **auf Englisch, auf Deutsch** there are the "3 K's."

Kinder

Küche

Kirche

Study **das** *(bilt)* **Bild** below *(oont)* **und** *(don)* **dann** write out **die** *(noy-en)* **neuen** *(vur-tair)* **Wörter** in the blanks on the next **Seite.**

(stahm-baum)
der Stammbaum
family tree

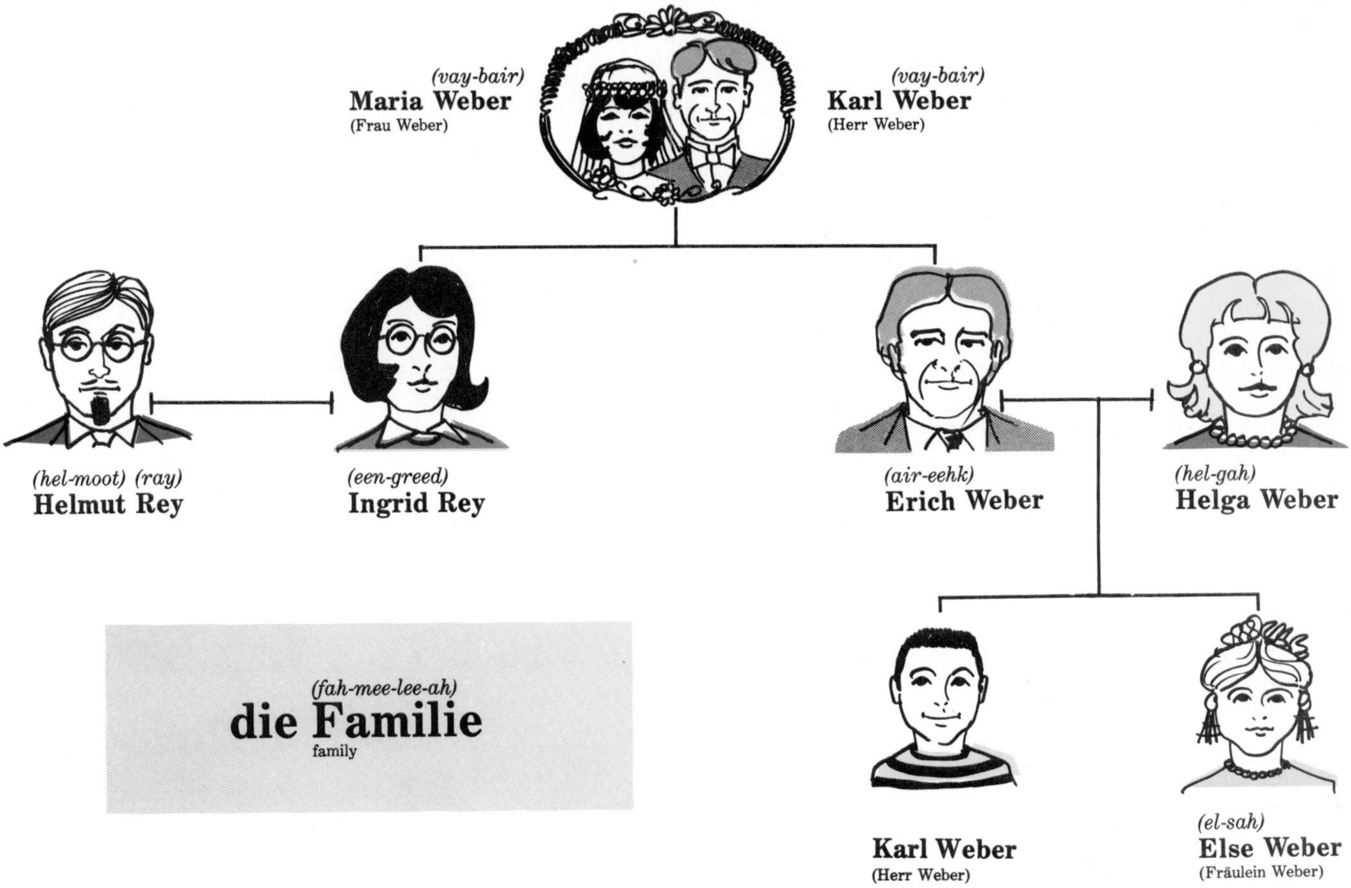

(vay-bair)
Maria Weber
(Frau Weber)

(vay-bair)
Karl Weber
(Herr Weber)

(hel-moot) (ray)
Helmut Rey

(een-greed)
Ingrid Rey

(air-eehk)
Erich Weber

(hel-gah)
Helga Weber

(fah-mee-lee-ah)
die Familie
family

Karl Weber
(Herr Weber)

(el-sah)
Else Weber
(Fräulein Weber)

☐ **kosten** *(koh-sten)*	to cost	________________
— ex. **Es kostet 10 Mark.**		________________
☐ **das Kotelett** *(koh-te-let)*	cutlet	________________
☐ **kühl** *(kewl)*	cool	________________
☐ **der Kühlschrank** *(kewl-shrahnk)*	cool closet/refrigerator	________________

die Großeltern *(grohs-el-tairn)* grandparents

die Eltern *(el-tairn)* parents

der Großvater *(grohs-fah-tair)* grandfather der Großvater

die Großmutter *(grohs-moo-tair)* grandmother ______

der Vater *(fah-tair)* father ______

die Mutter *(moo-tair)* mother ______

die Kinder *(kin-dair)* children

die Verwandten *(fair-vahn-ten)* relatives

der Sohn *(zohn)* son ______

die Tochter *(tohk-tair)* daughter ______

der Onkel *(ohn-kel)* uncle ______

die Tante *(tahn-tah)* aunt ______

Der Sohn und die Tochter sind auch Bruder *(broo-dair)* brother **und Schwester!** *(shves-tair)* sister

Let's learn how to identify **die Familie** *(fah-mee-lee-ah)* family by **Name** *(nah-mah)* name. Study the following examples.

Wie how **heißt** *(heist)* is called **der** *(dair)* the **Vater?** father

Der Vater heißt is called Erich.

Wie heißt *(heist)* is called **die** *(dee)* **Mutter?**

Die Mutter heißt is called Helga.

Nun you fill in the following blanks, based on the **Bilder,** in the same manner.

Wie heißt der Sohn?

______ **heißt** ______.

Wie heißt ______?

______ **heißt** Else.

Wie heißt ______?

______ **heißt** ______.

Wie heißt ______?

______ **heißt** ______.

- ☐ **landen** *(lahn-den)* .... to land ______
- ☐ **das Lamm** *(lahm)* .... lamb ______
- ☐ **die Lampe** *(lahm-pah)* .... lamp ______
- ☐ **das Land** *(lahnt)* .... land/country ______
- ☐ **die Landmarke** *(lahnt-mar-kah)* .... landmark ______

die Küche *(kew-sha)*
kitchen

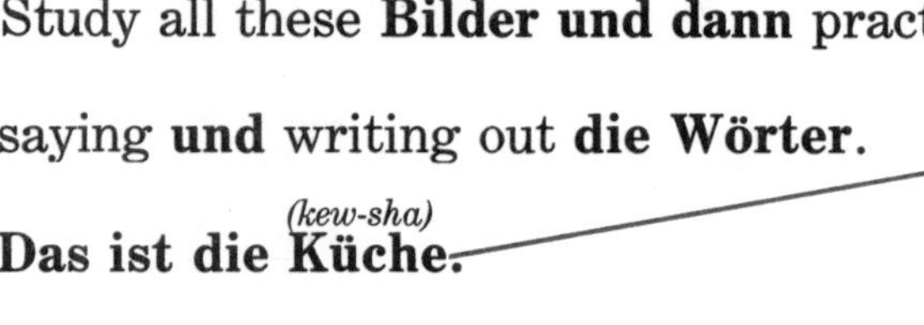

Study all these **Bilder** *(bil-dair)* **und dann** *(don)* practice saying **und** writing out **die Wörter**.

Das ist die Küche *(kew-sha)*.

der Kühlschrank *(dair) (kewl-shrahnk)*

der Kühlschrank

der Ofen / der Herd *(oh-fen) (hairt)*

der Wein *(vine)*

das Bier *(beer)*

die Milch *(milsh)*

die Butter *(boo-tair)*

Answer these questions aloud.

Wo *(voh)* **ist das Bier?** . . . . **Das Bier ist in dem Kühlschrank.**

Wo ist die *(dee)* **Milch?** **Wo ist der Wein?** **Wo ist die Butter?**

- ☐ **die Landung** *(lahn-doong)* . . . . landing ____________
- ☐ **lang** *(lahng)* . . . . long (vs. short = **kurz**) ____________
- ☐ **laut** *(lout)* . . . . loud (vs. soft = **leise**) ____________
- ☐ **lernen** *(lair-nen)* . . . . to learn ____________
- ☐ **das Licht** *(leeht)* . . . . light ____________

(oont) (mair)
Und mehr . . .
more

das Brot

Wo(voh) **ist das Brot? Das Brot ist in dem Schrank**(shrahnk)**. Wo ist der Tee**(tay)**? Wo ist der Kaffee**(kah-fay)**?** **Nun öffnen**(urf-nen) (open) your **Buch**(boohk) to the **Seite**(zigh-tah) **mit** the labels **und** remove the next **neunzehn**(noyn-tsayn) labels **und** proceed to label all these **Dinge** in your **Küche**(kew-sha)**.** Do not forget to use every opportunity to say these **Wörter** out loud. **Das ist sehr**(zair) **wichtig**(veehk-teeg) (important)**.**

- ☐ **der Likör** *(lee-kur)* . . . . liqueur ______
- ☐ **die Limonade** *(lee-moh-nah-dah)* . . . . . . lemonade ______
- ☐ **die Linie** *(lee-nee-ah)* . . . . line ______
- ☐ **die Lokomotive** *(loh-koh-moh-tee-vah)* . . locomotive ______
- ☐ **das Luxemburg** *(loox-em-boorg)* . . . . Luxembourg ______

die Kirche *(kirh-ha)* — church

In Deutschland, there **ist** not the wide variety of **Religionen** *(ray-lee-gee-ohn-en)* [religions] that **wir** *(vir)* [we] **finden** *(fin-den)* [find] **hier in Amerika**. A person's **Religion** *(ray-lee-gee-ohn)* **ist** usually one of the following.

1. **evangelisch** *(eh-vahn-gay-lish)* — Protestant ___evangelisch___
2. **katholisch** *(kah-toh-lish)* — Catholic ____________
3. **jüdisch** *(yew-dish)* — Jewish ____________

Hier ist eine Kirche *(kirh-ha)* **in Deutschland** *(doych-lahnt)***. Ist das eine katholische** *(kah-toh-lish-ah)* **oder evangelische** *(ay-vahn-gay-lish-ah)* **Kirche? Ist das eine neue** *(noy-ah)* **Kirche? Nein** *(nine)***, das ist eine sehr alte** *(ahl-tah)* [old] **Kirche.** You will see **viele** *(feel-ah)* [many] **schöne** *(shurn-ah)* [pretty] **Kirchen** *(kirh-hen)* like this during your holiday **in Deutschland.**

Nun let's learn how to say "I am" **auf Deutsch:** I am = **ich bin** *(eehk)* ____________

Practice saying **„ich bin"** **mit** the following **Wörtern** *(vur-tairn)*. **Nun** write each sentence for more practice.

Ich bin katholisch. ____________ **Ich bin evangelisch.** ____________

Ich bin jüdisch. ___Ich bin jüdisch.___ **Ich bin Amerikaner** *(ah-mair-ih-kahn-air)*. ____________

Ich bin in Europa *(oy-roh-pah)*. ____________ **Ich bin in Deutschland.** ____________

- ☐ **der Mai** *(my)* . . . . May ____________
- ☐ **der Mann** *(mahn)* . . . . man ____________
- ☐ **der Markt** *(markt)* . . . . market ____________
  — usually an open-air market in the town square ____________
- ☐ **die Marmelade** *(mahr-mih-lah-dah)* . . . . marmalade ____________

Ich bin in der *(kirh-ha)* **Kirche.** ____________ Ich bin in der *(kew-sha)* **Küche.** ____________

Ich bin die *(moo-tair)* **Mutter.** Ich bin die Mutter. Ich bin der *(fah-tair)* **Vater.** ____________

Ich bin in *(daim)* **dem Hotel.** ____________ Ich bin in dem Restaurant. ____________

Ich bin *(hoon-grig)* **hungrig** (hungry). ____________ Ich bin *(dur-stig)* **durstig** (thirsty). ____________

Nun identify all **die** *(pair-zoh-nen)* **Personen** (people) **in dem Bild** below by writing **das** *(reeh-tee-gah)* **richtige** (correct) **deutsche Wort** for each person on the line with the corresponding number *(oon-tair)* **unter dem Bild.**

1. ____________ 2. ____________

3. ____________ 4. ____________

5. der Onkel 6. ____________

7. ____________

- ☐ **der Mechaniker** *(may-kahn-ee-kair)*.... mechanic ____________
- ☐ **die Meile** *(my-lah)*.................. mile ____________
  — 1 mile = 1.67 **Kilometer** ____________
- ☐ **der Meter** *(may-tair)*................ meter ____________
  — **Ein Meter ist** about 1 yard; a **Kilometer ist 1000 Meter.** ____________

Step 11

You **haben** already used the verbs **haben** *(hah-ben)* **und möchten** *(murk-ten)*, **kosten** *(koh-sten)* (to cost), **finden, kochen** *(kohk-hen)* (to cook), **kommen** *(koh-men)*, **gehen, ist, sind, und bin.** Although you might be able to "get by" **mit** these verbs, let's assume you want to do **besser** *(bess-air)* (better) than that. First a quick review.

How do you say "I" **auf Deutsch?** ich How do you say "we" **auf Deutsch?** ____

Compare these **zwei** *(tsvai)* charts **sehr** carefully **und** learn these **sieben Wörter** on the right.

I	=	**ich** *(eehk)*
he	=	**er** *(air)*
she	=	**sie** *(zee)*
it	=	**es** *(es)*

we	=	**wir** *(vir)*
you	=	**Sie** *(zee)*
they	=	**sie** *(zee)*

Nun draw lines between the matching **englische und deutsche Wörter** *(vur-tair)* below to see if you can keep these **Wörter** straight in your mind.

wir	I
es	you
er	he
sie	we
ich	she
Sie	it
sie	they

Nun close **das Buch und** write out both columns of the above practice on **ein Stück** *(shtewk)* **Papier** *(pah-peer)*. How did **Sie** do? **Gut** *(goot)* **oder schlecht** *(shleckt)* (bad)? **Gut** *(goot)* **oder nicht so** *(zoh)* **gut? Nun** that **Sie** know these **Wörter, Sie** can say almost anything **auf Deutsch** with one basic formula: the "plug-in" formula. With this formula, you can correctly use any **Wörter Sie** wish.

- ☐ **mehr** *(mair)* . . . . more ________
- ☐ **die Milch** *(milsh)* . . . . milk ________
- ☐ **die Mitte** *(mit-tah)* . . . . middle ________
- ☐ **der Montag** *(mohn-tahk)* . . . . Monday ________
- ☐ **der Morgen** *(more-gen)* . . . . morning ________

To demonstrate, let's take *(zex)* **sechs** basic **und** practical verbs **und** see how the "plug-in" formula works. Write **die Verben** (verbs) in the blanks below after **Sie haben** practiced saying them.

(koh-men) **kommen** = to come	*(gay-en)* **gehen** = to go	*(lair-nen)* **lernen** = to learn
kommen	________________	________________
(brow-ken) **brauchen** = to need	*(hah-ben)* **haben** = to have	*(murk-ten)* **möchten** = would like
________________	________________	________________

Study the following verb patterns carefully.

(eehk) **ich**	*(koh-mah)* **komme**	= I *come*
	(gay-ah) **gehe**	= I *go*
	(lair-nah) **lerne**	= I *learn*
	(brow-kah) **brauche**	= I *need*
	(hah-bah) **habe**	= I *have*
	(murk-tah) **möchte**	= I *would like*

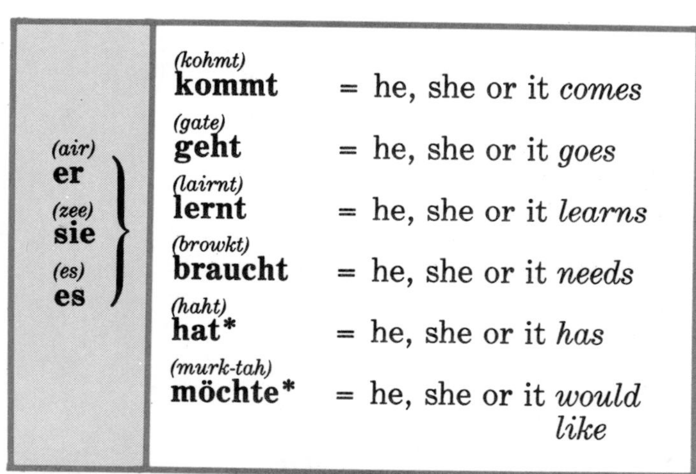

(air) **er** / *(zee)* **sie** / *(es)* **es**	*(kohmt)* **kommt**	= he, she or it *comes*
	(gate) **geht**	= he, she or it *goes*
	(lairnt) **lernt**	= he, she or it *learns*
	(browkt) **braucht**	= he, she or it *needs*
	(haht) **hat***	= he, she or it *has*
	(murk-tah) **möchte***	= he, she or it *would like*

Note:
- With **ich** you drop the final "n" from the basic verb form.
- With **er, sie,** or **es** you drop the final "en" of the basic verb form and substitute "t" instead.

*Some **Verben** just will not conform to the rules! But don't worry . . . you will be perfectly understood whether you say **„hat"** or **„habt."** Germans will be delighted that you have taken the time to learn the language.

- ☐ **der Mund** *(moont)*.................... mouth ________________
- ☐ **das Museum** *(moo-zay-oom)*........... museum ________________
- ☐ **die Musik** *(moo-zeek)*................ music ________________
- ☐ **die Mutter** *(moo-tair)*............... mother ________________
- ☐ **nächst** *(nexst)*...................... next ________________

With *(vir)* „**wir**," (we) *(zee)* „**Sie**," (you) or *(zee)* „**sie**," (they) there is no change at all!

wir / Sie / sie					
	kommen	= we, you, or they *come*	**brauchen**	= we, you, or they *need*
	gehen	= we, you, or they *go*	**haben**	= we, you, or they *have*
	lernen	= we, you, or they *learn*	**möchten**	= we, you, or they *would like*

Note: **Sie** only **haben zwei** changes to remember.

ich is followed by verbs with an "e" on the end . . . . *ex.* **ich brauche**

er, sie, es are followed by verbs with a "t" on the end . . . . *ex.* **er braucht** / **sie braucht** / **es braucht**

Deutsche verbs are easy. At the back of **das** *(boohk)* **Buch,** *(zee)* **Sie** will find *(zee-ben)* **sieben** *(zigh-ten)* **Seiten** of flash cards to help **Sie** learn these *(noy-ah)* **neue** *(vur-tair)* **Wörter.** Cut them out, carry them in your briefcase, purse, pocket *(oh-dair)* **oder** knapsack; *(oont)* **und** review them whenever **Sie** *(hah-ben)* **haben** a free moment.

Nun fill in the following blanks **mit** the correct form of the verb shown. Each time **Sie** write out the sentence, be sure *(owk)* **auch** to say it aloud.

(lair-nen) **lernen** — to learn

Ich ____________ *(doych)* **Deutsch.**

Er / Sie / Es lernt **Deutsch.**

Wir ____________ **Deutsch.**

Sie (you) ____________ *(eng-leash)* **Englisch.**

Sie (they) ____________ **Deutsch.**

(koh-men) **kommen** — to come

Ich ____________ **aus** *(ah-mair-ih-kah)* **Amerika.**

Er / Sie / Es ____________ **aus Amerika.**

Wir ____________ **aus** *(hole-lahnt)* **Holland.**

Sie (you) kommen **aus** *(eng-lahnt)* **England.**

Sie (they) ____________ **aus Deutschland.**

- ☐ **die Nacht** *(nahkt)* . . . . night ____________
  — ex. **„Gute Nacht!"**
- ☐ **der Name** *(nah-mah)* . . . . name ____________
- ☐ **die Nation** *(nah-tsi-ohn)* . . . . nation ____________
- ☐ **die Nationalität** *(nah-tsi-oh-nahl-ih-tate)* nationality ____________

(gay-en)
gehen
to go

Ich ________ **nach Deutschland.**
Er
Sie ________ **nach Italien.**
Es
Wir ________ **nach Holland.**

Sie (you) ________ **nach England.**

Sie (they) gehen **nach China.**

(brow-ken)
brauchen
to need

Ich ________ **ein** (tsi-mair) **Zimmer.**
Er
Sie ________ **ein Zimmer.**
Es
Wir brauchen **ein Zimmer.**

Sie (you) ________ **ein Zimmer.**

Sie (they) ________ **ein Zimmer.**

(hah-ben)
haben
to have

Ich habe **fünf Mark.**
Er
Sie ________ **sechs Mark.**
Es
Wir ________ **zehn Mark.**

Sie (you) ________ **zwei Mark.**

Sie (they) ________ **drei Mark.**

(murk-ten)
möchten
would like

Ich ________ **ein Glas Wein.**
Er
Sie ________ **eine** (tah-sah) **Tasse** (cup) (kah-kow) **Kakao.** (hot chocolate)
Es
Wir ________ **ein Glas Weißwein.**

Sie (you) ________ **ein Glas Milch.**

Sie (they) möchten **ein Glas Bier.**

Hier sind (zex) **sechs** more **Verben.**

(high-sen) **heißen** = to be called
____

(kow-fen) **kaufen** = to buy
____

(shprek-en) **sprechen** = to speak
____

(voh-nen) **wohnen** = to live/reside
____

(be-stel-en) **bestellen** = to order
____

(bly-ben) **bleiben** = to stay/remain
bleiben

- ☐ **natürlich** *(nah-tewr-leehk)* .... naturally ________
- ☐ **der November** *(noh-vem-bair)*.......... November ________
- ☐ **die Nummer** *(noo-mair)*........... number ________
- ☐ **der Ofen** *(oh-fen)*................. oven ________
- ☐ **oft** *(ohft)*......................... often ________

Nun, fill in the following blanks **mit** the correct form of each verb. Be sure to say each sentence out loud until **Sie haben es** down pat!

(high-sen)
heißen
to be called

Ich ______________ **Doktor Müller.**

Er
Sie ______________ **Zimmermann.**
Es

Wir ______________ **Faber.**

Sie (you) ______________ **Holtzheimer.**

Sie (they) *heißen* **Familie Nickel.**

(kow-fen)
kaufen
to buy

Ich *kaufe* **ein Buch.**

Er
Sie ______________ **einen Salat.**
Es

Wir ______________ **ein Auto.**

Sie (you) ______________ **eine Uhr.**

Sie (they) ______________ **eine Lampe.**

(shprek-en)
sprechen
to be called

Ich ______________ **Deutsch.**

Er
Sie ______________ **Englisch.**
Es

Wir ______________ **Spanisch.**

Sie (you) *sprechen* **Dänisch.**

Sie (they) ______________ **Japanisch.**

(voh-nen)
wohnen
to live/reside

Ich *wohne* **in Deutschland.**

Er
Sie ______________ **in Amerika.**
Es

Wir ______________ **in einem Hotel.**

Sie (you) ______________ **in Europa.**

Sie (they) ______________ **in Japan.**

(be-stel-en)
bestellen
to order

Ich ______________ **ein Glas Wasser.**

Er
Sie ______________ **ein Glas Wein.**
Es

Wir *bestellen* **eine Tasse Tee.**

Sie (you) ______________ **eine Tasse Kaffee.**

Sie (they) ______________ **ein Glas Milch.**

(bly-ben)
bleiben
to stay/remain

Ich ______________ **noch** *(nohk)* still **fünf Tage.**

Er
Sie *bleibt* **noch drei Tage.**
Es

Wir ______________ **noch sechs Tage.**

Sie (you) ______________ **noch sieben Tage.**

Sie (they) ______________ **noch acht Tage.**

☐ **offen** *(ohf-fen)*. . . . . open ______________
— ex. **Das Restaurant ist offen.** ______________
☐ **der Offizier** *(oh-fih-tseer)*. . . . . officer ______________
— ex. **Der Offizier ist um die Ecke.** ______________
☐ **der Oktober** *(ohk-toh-bair)*. . . . . October ______________

Nun see if **Sie** *(zee)* can fill in the blanks below. The correct answers **sind** *(zint)* at the bottom of the **Seite** *(zigh-tah)*.

1. I speak German. ________________
2. He comes from America. ________________
3. We learn German. ________________
4. They have 10 marks. ________________
5. She would like a glass of water. ________________
6. We need a room. ________________
7. I am called Faber. ________________
8. I live in America. ________________
9. You are buying a book. Sie kaufen ein Buch.
10. He orders a beer. ________________

In the following Steps, **Sie** *(zee)* will be introduced to more **und** more **Verben und** should drill them in exactly the same way as **Sie** did in this section. Look up **neue Wörter** in your **Wörterbuch** *(vur-tair-boohk)* (dictionary) **und** make up your own sentences using the same type of pattern. Remember, the more **Sie** practice **nun**, the more enjoyable your trip will be. **Viel Glück!**

Nun ist a perfect time to turn to the back of **das Buch,** clip out your flash cards, and start flashing.

Be sure to check off your free **Wörter** in the box provided as **Sie lernen** each one. 

ANTWORTEN

1. **Ich spreche Deutsch.**
2. **Er kommt aus Amerika.**
3. **Wir lernen Deutsch.**
4. **Sie haben zehn Mark.**
5. **Sie möchte ein Glas Wasser.**
6. **Wir brauchen ein Zimmer.**
7. **Ich heiße Faber.**
8. **Ich wohne in Amerika.**
9. **Sie kaufen ein Buch.**
10. **Er bestellt ein Bier.**

(mih-noo-ten) die Minuten
minutes

Step 12

Sie know (vee) **wie** to tell **die** (tah-gah) **Tage** of the (voh-kah) **Woche und die** (moh-nah-tah) **Monate** of the **Jahr,** so **nun** let's learn to tell time. Punctuality **in Deutschland ist sehr** (veehk-teeg) **wichtig,** not to mention the need of catching (tsew-gah) **Züge** (trains) **und** arriving on time. **Hier sind** the "basics."

What time is it?	=	(vee) (shpayt) **Wie spät ist es?**
		(vee-feel) (uhr) **Wieviel Uhr ist es?**

before	=	(for) **vor**	vor
after	=	(nahk) **nach**	______
half	=	(hahlp) **halb**	______

Es ist (fewnf) **fünf Uhr.**

Es ist (hahlp) **halb fünf.**

Es ist (dry) **drei Uhr.**

Es ist halb drei.

Es ist (tsvahn-tsig) **zwanzig Minuten** (nahk) **nach** (ahkt) **acht.** **ODER** **Es ist acht Uhr zwanzig.**

Es ist zwanzig Minuten (for) **vor acht.** **ODER** **Es ist** (zee-ben) **sieben Uhr** (fear-tsig) **vierzig.**

Nun fill in the blanks according to the (tsight) **Zeit** (time) indicated on the (uhr) **Uhr** (clock). The answers **sind** below.

Es ist ______________________.

Es ist ______________________.

Es ist ______________________.

Es ist ______________________.

Es ist ______________________.

Es ist vier Uhr.

Es ist ______________________.

Es ist ______________________.

ANTWORTEN

Es ist zehn Uhr zehn.
Es ist zwanzig Minuten nach zwei.
Es ist halb acht.
Es ist sechs Uhr zehn.
(Es ist zehn Minuten nach sechs.)

Es ist halb zwei.
Es ist vier Uhr.
Es ist zwanzig Minuten nach zwölf.
Es ist zehn Minuten vor sechs.
(Es ist fünf Uhr fünfzig.)

Hier sind more time-telling **Wörter** to add to your **Wort** power.

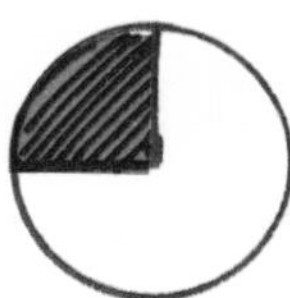

ein *(fear-tel)* **Viertel**	=	a quarter
ein Viertel vor	=	a quarter before
ein Viertel nach	=	a quarter after

Es ist ein *(fear-tel)* **Viertel nach** *(tsvai)* **zwei.** <u>**ODER**</u> **Es ist zwei Uhr** *(fewnf-tsayn)* **fünfzehn.**

Es ist ein Viertel vor zwei. <u>**ODER**</u> **Es ist ein Uhr** *(fewnf-oont-fear-tsig)* **fünfundvierzig.**

Nun es ist your turn.

Es ist ______________________.

Es ist ______________________.

Es ist ein Viertel vor drei.

Es ist ______________________.

See how *(veehk-teeg)* **wichtig** (important) learning **die Nummern ist? Nun** answer the following *(frah-gen)* **Fragen** (questions) based on the **Uhren** below. The answers **sind** at the bottom of the **Seite**.

***(vee)* Wie *(shpayt)* spät ist es?**

1. Es ist sechs Uhr.
2. ______________________
3. ______________________
4. ______________________
5. ______________________
6. ______________________
7. ______________________

ANTWORTEN

1. **Es ist sechs Uhr.**
2. **Es ist halb acht.**
   Es ist sieben Uhr dreißig.
3. **Es ist acht Uhr.**
4. **Es ist halb zwei.**
   Es ist ein Uhr dreißig.
5. **Es ist ein Viertel nach zwölf.**
   Es ist zwölf Uhr fünfzehn.
6. **Es ist zwanzig Minuten nach neun.**
   Es ist vierzig Minuten vor zehn.
7. **Es ist siebzehn Minuten nach zwei.**
   Es ist dreiundvierzig Minuten vor drei.

When **Sie** *(zee)* answer a „**Wann**“ *(vahn)* question, say „**um**“ *(oom)* (at) before you give the time.

ZUG 43 | 6:00

Wann *(vahn)* **kommt der Zug** *(tsook)***?** um sechs Uhr.

Nun answer the following **Fragen** *(frah-gen)* based on the **Uhren** below. Be sure to practice saying each question out loud several times.

Wann *(vahn)* **beginnt** *(bay-gint)* **das Konzert** *(kohn-tsairt)***?** __________.

Wann beginnt das Theater *(tay-ah-tair)***?** __________.

Wann kommt der *(dair)* **gelbe Bus** *(boos)***?** __________.

Wann kommt das Taxi *(tahx-ee)***?** um halb fünf.

Wann *(vahn)* **ist das Restaurant auf** *(owf)* (open)**?** __________.

Wann ist das Restaurant zu *(tsoo)* (closed)**?** __________.

Um *(oom)* (at) **acht Uhr morgens sagt** *(zahkt)* (says) **man** *(mahn)* (one)**,**
„Guten Morgen, Frau (Mrs.) **Bernhard!“**

Um *(oom)* (at) **acht Uhr abends sagt man,**
„Guten Abend, Fräulein *(froy-line)* (Miss) **Seehafer!”**

Um *(oom)* **ein Uhr nachmittags** *(nahk-mit-tahgs)* **sagt man,**
„Guten Tag, Herr *(hair)* (Mr.) **Richter** *(reek-tair)***!“**

Um *(oom)* **zehn Uhr abends sagt man,**
„Gute *(goo-tah)* **Nacht!“**

- ☐ **das Ohr** *(or)* .... ear __________
- ☐ **der Ohrring** *(or-ring)* .... earring __________
- ☐ **das Öl** *(url)* .... oil __________
- ☐ **das Omelett** *(oh-mih-let)* .... omelette __________
- ☐ **der Onkel** *(ohn-kel)* .... uncle __________

Remember:

What time is it? =	**Wie spät ist es?** / **Wieviel Uhr ist es?**

When/at what time =	**Wann** / **Um wieviel Uhr**

Can **Sie** pronounce **und** understand the following paragraph?

Der Zug von Stuttgart kommt um 15:15. Es ist nun 15:20. Der Zug *(tsook)* ist spät. Der Zug *(tsook)* kommt heute um 17:15. Morgen kommt der Zug wieder *(vee-dair)* (again) um 15:15.

Hier sind more practice exercises. Answer **die Fragen** *(frah-gen)* (questions) based on the **Zeit** *(tsight)* given.

Wieviel Uhr ist es?

1. (10:30) ____________________
2. (6:30) ____________________
3. (2:15) ____________________
4. (11:40) Es ist elf Uhr vierzig.
5. (12:18) ____________________
6. (7:20) ____________________
7. (3:10) ____________________
8. (4:05) ____________________
9. (5:35) ____________________
10. (11:50) ____________________

☐ **die Oper** *(oh-pair)*.................. opera
— ex. **Ich gehe in die Oper.**
☐ **das Opernhaus** *(oh-pairn-house)*....... opera house
— ex. **Das Opernhaus ist sehr groß.**
☐ **die Ordnung** *(ohrd-noong)*............ order

(here) **Hier ist** a quick quiz. Fill in the blanks **mit den** *(reehk-tee-gen)* **richtigen** (correct) **Nummern.** The answers **sind unten.**

1. **Eine Minute hat** ______ (?) *(zay-koon-den)* **Sekunden.** (seconds)
2. **Eine Stunde** (hour) **hat** ______ (?) **Minuten.**
3. **Ein Tag hat** ______ (?) *(shtoon-den)* **Stunden.** (hours)
4. **Eine Woche hat** sieben (?) **Tage.**
5. **Ein** *(moh-naht)* **Monat hat** ______ (?) *(tah-gah)* **Tage.**
6. **Ein Jahr hat** ______ (?) **Monate.**
7. **Ein Jahr hat** ______ (?) *(voh-ken)* **Wochen.**
8. **Ein Jahr hat** ______ (?) **Tage.**

Hier ist a sample **Seite von** *(ine-em)* **einem deutschen Zugfahrplan** (train schedule). **Ein** *(tay-ay-ay)* **TEE-Zug ist sehr schnell** (fast). **Ein** *(day)* **D-Zug ist schnell, und ein** *(ay)* **E-Zug ist** *(long-zahm)* **langsam** (slow). Which **Zug** would **Sie** prefer to take?

von Heidelberg nach Frankfurt

(ahp) **ab** leaves	**Zug #**	*(on)* **an** arrives	*(bih-mair-koong-en)* **Bemerkungen** notes
7:40	TEE 40	8:30	
10:00	D 16	11:10	
12:15	D 38	13:25	
14:32	E 693	16:15	

ANTWORTEN

1. **sechzig**
2. **sechzig**
3. **vierundzwanzig**
4. **sieben**
5. **dreißig**
6. **zwölf**
7. **zweiundfünfzig**
8. **dreihundert-fünfundsechzig**

Hier sind die *(noy-en)* **neuen Verben für** Step 12.

(zah-gen) **sagen** = to say	*(es-sen)* **essen** = to eat	*(trink-en)* **trinken** = to drink
______________	essen	______________

(zah-gen) **sagen**
to say

Ich ______________ **das** *(hoy-tah)* **heute.**

Er
Sie ______________ *(feel)* **viel** (much) **heute.**
Es

Wir sagen **„nein."** *(nine)* (no)

Sie ______________ **„ja."** (yes)

Sie ______________ *(neehk-ts)* **nichts.** (nothing)

(es-sen) **essen**
to eat

Ich ______________ *(vee-nair)* **Wiener** *(shnit-tsel)* **Schnitzel.**

Er
Sie ______________ *(fish)* **Fisch.**
Es

Wir ______________ **eine** *(zoo-pah)* **Suppe.** (soup)

Sie (you) essen **ein Beefsteak.**

Sie (they) ______________ *(lahm)* **Lamm.** (lamb)

(trink-en) **trinken**
to drink

Ich ______________ *(milsh)* **Milch.**

Er
Sie trinkt *(vice-vine)* **Weißwein.**
Es

Wir ______________ **Mineralwasser.**

Sie ______________ *(toh-mah-ten-zahft)* **Tomatensaft.** (tomato juice)

Sie ______________ *(kah-kow)* **Kakao.** (hot chocolate)

Remember that **„ei"** is pronounced like "eye" or like the "i" in "mine."

- ☐ **das Orchester** *(or-kes-tair)* . . . . orchestra ______________
  — ex. **Das Orchester in New York ist sehr groß.** ______________
- ☐ **die Organization** *(ohr-gahn-ih-zah-tsi-ohn)* . . organization ______________
- ☐ **die Orgel** *(or-gell)* . . . . organ ______________
  — ex. **Die Orgel ist sehr alt.** ______________

(bilt)
das **Bild**
(deck-ah)
die **Decke**
(eck-ah)
die **Ecke**
(fen-stair)
das **Fenster**
(lahm-pah)
die **Lampe**
(leeht)
das **Licht**
(zoh-fah)
das **Sofa**
(shtool)
der **Stuhl**
(tep-eeh)
der **Teppich**
(tish)
der **Tisch**
(tewr)
die **Tür**
(uhr)
die **Uhr**
(for-hahng)
der **Vorhang**
(vahnt)
die **Wand**
(house)
das **Haus**
(es-tsi-mair)
das **Eßzimmer**
(vohn-tsi-mair)
das **Wohnzimmer**
(shlahf-tsi-mair)
das **Schlafzimmer**
(bah-da-tsi-mair)
das **Badezimmer**
(kew-sha)
die **Küche**

(bew-roh)
das **Büro**
(kel-lair)
der **Keller**
(ga-rah-zha)
die **Garage**
(ow-toe)
das **Auto**
(vah-gen)
der **Wagen**
(fahr-raht)
das **Fahrrad**
(hoont)
der **Hund**
(kaht-tsa)
die **Katze**
(gar-ten)
der **Garten**
(bloo-men)
die **Blumen**
(breef-kah-sten)
der **Briefkasten**
(post)
die **Post**
(kling-el)
die **Klingel**
(ines)
1 eins
(tsvai)
2 zwei
(dry)
3 drei
(fear)
4 vier
(fewnf)
5 fünf
(zex)
6 sechs
(zee-ben)
7 sieben

(ahkt)
8 acht
(noyn)
9 neun
(tsayn)
10 zehn
(vice)
weiß
(shvarts)
schwarz
(gelp)
gelb
(roht)
rot
(blau)
blau
(grau)
grau
(brown)
braun
(grewn)
grün
(roh-zah)
rosa
(boont)
bunt
(zohn-tahk)
der **Sonntag**
(mohn-tahk)
der **Montag**
(deens-tahk)
der **Dienstag**
(mit-vohk)
der **Mittwoch**
(doh-nairs-tahk)
der **Donnerstag**
(fry-tahk)
der **Freitag**
(zahms-tahk)
der **Samstag**

(goo-ten) (more-gen)
Guten Morgen
(goo-ten) (tahk)
Guten Tag
(goo-ten) (ah-bent)
Guten Abend
(goo-tah) (nahkt)
Gute Nacht
(kewl-shrahnk)
der **Kühlschrank**
(oh-fen)
der **Ofen**
(vine)
der **Wein**
(beer)
das **Bier**
(milsh)
die **Milch**
(boo-tair)
die **Butter**
(tell-air)
der **Teller**
(mes-sair)
das **Messer**
(gah-bel)
die **Gabel**
(lur-fel)
der **Löffel**
(zair-vee-et-tah)
die **Serviette**
(tah-sah)
die **Tasse**
(glahs)
das **Glas**
(zahlts)
das **Salz**
(fef-air)
der **Pfeffer**
(shrahnk)
der **Schrank**

STICKY LABELS

This book has over 150 special sticky labels for you to use as you learn new words. When you are introduced to a word, remove the corresponding label from these pages. Be sure to use each of these unique labels by adhering them to a picture, window, lamp, or whatever object it refers to. The sticky labels make learning to speak German much more fun and a lot easier than you ever expected.

For example, when you look in the mirror and see the label, say

(dair) *(shpee-gel)*
"der Spiegel."

Don't just say it once, say it again and again.

And once you label the refrigerator, you should never again open that door without saying

(dair) *(kewl-shrahnk)*
"der Kühlschrank."

By using the sticky labels, you not only learn new words but friends and family learn along with you!

(broht) das Brot

(tay) der Tee

(kah-fay) der Kaffee

(vah-sair) das Wasser

(kah-kow) der Kakao

(bet) das Bett

(bet-deck-ah) ie Bettdecke

(kohpf-kiss-en) das Kopfkissen

(veck-air) der Wecker

(kly-dair-shrahnk) der Kleiderschrank

(vahsh-beck-en) as Waschbecken

(doosh-ah) die Dusche

(toy-let-tah) die Toilette

(toohk) das Tuch

(hahnt-toohk) as Handtuch

(bah-dah-toohk) das Badetuch

(vahsh-lah-pen) er Waschlappen

(shpee-gel) der Spiegel

(bly-shtift) der Bleistift

(koo-lee) der Kuli

(pah-peer) das Papier

(pah-peer-kohrp) der Papierkorb

(breef) der Brief

(breef-mahr-kah) die Briefmarke

(boohk) das Buch

(post-kar-tah) die Postkarte

(tsight-shrift) die Zeitschrift

(tsigh-toong) die Zeitung

(bril-ah) die Brille

(fairn-zay-air) der Fernseher

(pah-ss) der Paß

(flook-kar-tah) die Flugkarte

(gelt) das Geld

(kah-mair-ah) die Kamera

(film) der Film

(koh-fair) der Koffer

(breef-tah-shah) die Brieftasche

(hahnt-tah-shah) die Handtasche

(bah-da-on-tsook) der Badeanzug

(zahn-dah-len) die Sandalen

(zigh-fah) die Seife

(tsahn-bewr-stah) die Zahnbürste

(tsahn-pah-stah) die Zahnpaste

(kahm) der Kamm

(mahn-tel) der Mantel

(ray-gen-mahn-tel) der Regenmantel

(ray-gen-shirm) der Regenschirm

(hahnt-shoo-ah) die Handschuhe

(hoot) der Hut

(shoo-ah) die Schuhe

(shtee-fel) die Stiefel

(zoh-ken) die Socken

(shtroompf-hoh-zah) die Strumpfhose

(shlahf-on-tsook) der Schlafanzug

(nahkt-hemt) das Nachthemd

(house-shoo-ah) die Hausschuhe

(bah-da-mahn-tel) der Bademantel

(on-tsook) der Anzug

(krah-vah-tah) die Krawatte

(tah-shen-toohk) das Taschentuch

(yah-kah) die Jacke

(hoh-zah) die Hose

(hemt) das Hemd

(klite) das Kleid

(rohk) der Rock

(bloo-zah) die Bluse

(pool-ee) der Pulli

(oon-tair-hoh-zah) die Unterhose

(oon-tair-hemt) das Unterhemd

(oon-tair-rohk) der Unterrock

(bay-hah) der BH

(goo-ten) (ah-pe-teet) Guten Appetit!

(be-zetst) besetzt

(ent-shool-dee-goong) Entschuldigung

(eehk) (bin) (ah-mair-ih-kahn-air) Ich bin Amerikaner.

(eehk) (murk-tah) (doych) (lair-nen) Ich möchte Deutsch lernen.

(eehk) (high-sah) Ich heiße ____________.

PLUS . . .

Your book includes a number of other innovative features. At the back of the book, you'll find seven pages of flash cards. Cut them out and flip through them at least once a day.

On pages 112 and 113, you'll find a beverage guide and a menu guide. Don't wait until your trip to use them. Clip out the menu guide and use it tonight at the dinner table. And use the beverage guide to practice ordering your favorite drinks.

By using the special features in this book, you will be speaking German before you know it.

Nord - Süd, Ost - West

(nort) (zewt) (ohst) (vest)
north - south, east - west

Step 13

If **Sie** are looking at a **Landkarte** (lahnt-kar-tah) map **und Sie** see the following **Wörter**, **es** should **nicht** (neehkt) not be too difficult to figure out **was sie** (zee) they mean. Take an educated guess. The answers **sind** below.

(nort-zay) **die Nordsee**	(ohst-zay) **die Ostsee**	(ohst-bear-leen) **Ostberlin**
(nort-leehkt) **das Nordlicht**	(nort-kahp) **das Nordkap**	(vest-bear-leen) **Westberlin**
(nort-ah-mair-ih-kah) **das Nordamerika**	(zewt-ah-mair-ih-kah) **das Südamerika**	(zewt-pole) **der Südpol**
(nort-pole) **der Nordpol**	(ohst-ah-zee-en) **das Ostasien**	(zewt-ah-free-kah) **das Südafrika**

Die deutschen Wörter für north, south, east **und** west **sind** easy to recognize due to their similarity to **Englisch**. So . . .

(nor-den) **der Norden**	=	the north	__________
(zew-den) **der Süden**	=	the south	der Süden
(oh-sten) **der Osten**	=	the east	__________
(ves-ten) **der Westen**	=	the west	__________

(nurt-leehk) **nördlich**	=	northern	__________
(zewt-leehk) **südlich**	=	southern	__________
(ohst-leehk) **ostlich**	=	eastern	__________
(vest-leehk) **westlich**	=	western	westlich

Der Westen ist often the phrase used to refer to the American Wild West. **Der Osten** by comparison **ist** frequently used by West Germans when referring to East Germany.

But what about more basic directions such as "left," "right," "straight ahead" **und** "around the corner"? Let's learn these **Wörter nun**.

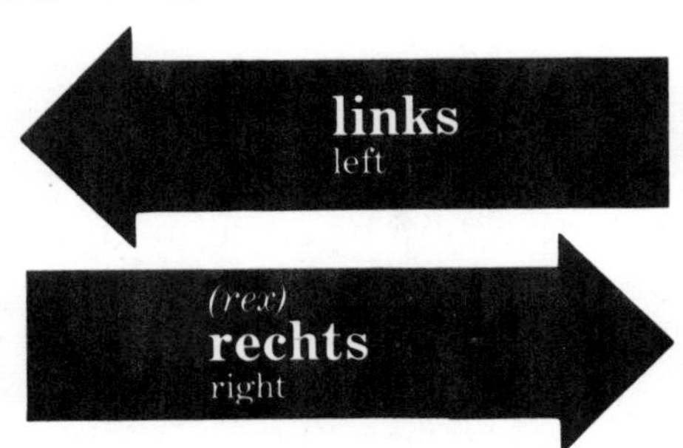

straight ahead	=	(ge-rah-dah-ows) **geradeaus**
around the corner	=	(oom) (eck-ah) **um die Ecke**
on the right side	=	(owf) (reck-ten) **auf der rechten Seite**
on the left side	=	**auf der linken Seite**

ANTWORTEN

the North Sea	the East Sea = Baltic Sea	East Berlin
the Northern Lights	the North Cap	West Berlin
North America	South America	the South Pole
the North Pole	East Asia	South Africa

Just as **auf Englisch**, these **drei Wörter** go a long way.

(bit-tah) **bitte**	=	please ________________
(dahn-kah) **danke**	=	thank you danke ________________
(ent-shool-dee-goong) **Entschuldigung**	=	excuse me ________________

Hier sind *(tsvai)* **zwei sehr** *(two-pish-ah)* **typische** (typical) *(kohn-fair-zah-tsi-oh-nen)* **Konversationen für** someone who is trying to find something.

Karl: *(ent-shool-dee-goong)* **Entschuldigung. Wo ist das Hotel** *(rih-tair)* **Ritter?** (knight)

Heinz: *(gay-en)* **Gehen** (go) **Sie zwei Straßen** *(vhy-tair)* **weiter,** (further) **dann links, dann geradeaus. Sie finden dann das Hotel Ritter.**

Karl: **Entschuldigung. Wo ist das Deutsche Museum?**

Helga: **Gehen Sie geradeaus und dann rechts um die Ecke.** *(oon-ge-fair)* **Ungefähr** (approximately) **hundert Meter** *(vhy-tair)* **weiter auf der linken Seite ist das Deutsche Museum.**

Are you lost? There is no need to be lost if **Sie haben** learned the basic direction **Wörter**. Do not try to memorize these **Konversationen** because you will never be looking for precisely these places! One day you might need to ask for directions to **„das Restaurant zur Sonne“ oder „das Goethe Museum“ oder „das Hotel Europa.“** Learn the key direction **Wörter** and be sure **Sie** can find your destination.

What if the person responding to your **Frage** answers too quickly for you to understand the entire reply? If so, ask again, saying,

- ☐ **der Ozean** *(oh-tsay-on)* . . . . ocean ________
  — ex. **Der Ozean ist blau und grün.** ________
- ☐ **ein paar** *(par)* . . . . a pair/a couple ________
- ☐ **packen** *(pah-ken)* . . . . to pack ________
- ☐ **das Paket** *(pah-kate)* . . . . package ________

Entschuldigung *(ent-shool-dee-goong)*. **Ich bin Amerikaner und ich spreche nur** *(noor)* only **ein** a **bißchen** *(bis-hen)* little **Deutsch.**

Sprechen speak **Sie bitte langsamer** *(long-zah-mair)* slower**. Wiederholen** *(vee-dair-hoh-len)* repeat **Sie das** that **bitte.**

Nun when the directions are repeated, **Sie** will be able to understand if **Sie haben** learned the key **Wörter** for directions. Quiz yourself by filling in the blanks below **mit den** *(dane)* **richtigen deutschen Wörtern**.

Liesel: **Entschuldigung. Wo ist das Restaurant Seeblick** *(zay-blick)* sea view**?**

Johannes: **Gehen** *(gay-en)* **Sie** _____ three _____ streets _____ further, **dann** *(don)* _____ left

um around _____ the _____ corner, **dann** _____ straight ahead.

Dort ist eine Kirche. Dann _____ right _____ around _____ the

_____ corner. Auf On _____ the _____ left _____ side

ist das Restaurant Seeblick *(zay-blick)* sea view**. Viel Glück.**

Hier sind vier neue Verben.

stehen *(shtay-en)* = to stand _____

verstehen *(fair-shtay-en)* = to understand _____

verkaufen *(fair-kow-fen)* = to sell verkaufen

wiederholen *(vee-dair-hoh-len)* = to repeat _____

- ☐ **das Papier** *(pah-peer)*. . . . . paper _____
- ☐ **der Park** *(park)*. . . . . park _____
- ☐ **der Passagier** *(pah-sa-zheer)*. . . . . passenger _____
- ☐ **der Paß** *(pah-ss)*. . . . . passport _____
- ☐ **die Paßkontrolle** *(pah-ss-kohn-troll-ah)* passport control _____

As always, say each sentence out loud. Say each and every **Wort** carefully, pronouncing everything **Sie** see.

(shtay-en)
stehen
to stand

Ich stehe **auf der linken Seite.**

Er
Sie _______________ **hinter dem Haus.**
Es

Wir _______________ **vor dem Haus.**

Sie (you) _______________ **neben dem Haus.**

Sie (they) _______________ **auf dem Haus.**

(fair-shtay-en)
verstehen
to understand

Ich _______________ **Deutsch.**

Er
Sie _______________ **Englisch.**
Es

Wir _______________ **Dänisch.**

Sie verstehen **Italienisch.**

Sie _______________ *(roo-sish)* **Russisch.**

(fair-kow-fen)
verkaufen
to sell

Ich _______________ **das Bett.**

Er
Sie _______________ **die grüne Jacke.**
Es

Wir _______________ **den neuen Film.**

Sie _______________ **den guten Fisch.**

Sie verkaufen **viele Karten.**

(vee-dair-hoh-len)
wiederholen
to repeat

Ich wiederhole **das Wort.**

Er
Sie _______________ **das nicht.**
Es

Wir _______________ **das Wort nicht.**

Sie _______________ **das.**

Sie _______________ **das nicht.**

Nun, see if **Sie** can translate the following thoughts into **Deutsch.** The answers **sind unten.**

1. She repeats the word. _______________
2. They sell tickets. Sie verkaufen Karten.
3. He stands in front of the house. _______________
4. We eat fish. _______________
5. I speak German. _______________
6. I drink tea. _______________

ANTWORTEN

1. **Sie wiederholt das Wort.**
2. **Sie verkaufen Karten.**
3. **Er steht vor dem Haus.**
4. **Wir essen Fisch.**
5. **Ich spreche Deutsch.**
6. **Ich trinke Tee.**

Step 14

(oh-ben) Oben - (oon-ten) Unten
above — below

Before **Sie beginnen** Step 14, review Step 8. (noon) **Nun** (lair-nen) **lernen** (vir) **wir mehr.**

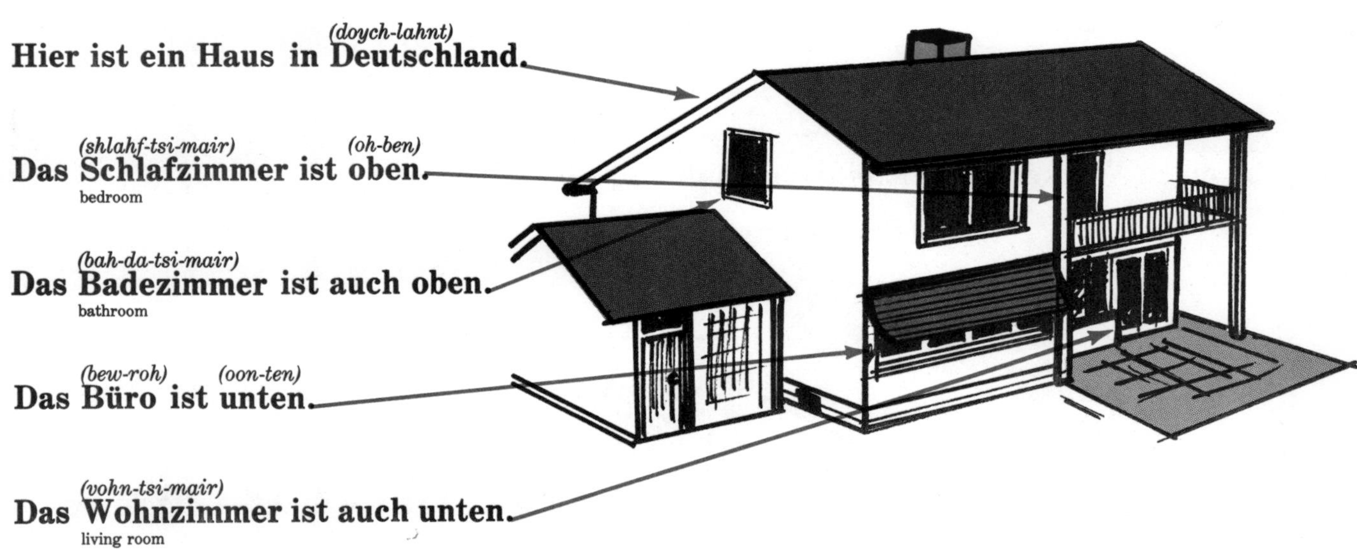

Hier ist ein Haus in (doych-lahnt) **Deutschland.**

Das (shlahf-tsi-mair) **Schlafzimmer** (bedroom) **ist** (oh-ben) **oben.**

Das (bah-da-tsi-mair) **Badezimmer** (bathroom) **ist auch oben.**

Das (bew-roh) **Büro ist** (oon-ten) **unten.**

Das (vohn-tsi-mair) **Wohnzimmer** (living room) **ist auch unten.**

(gay-en) **Gehen** (go) **Sie nun in** your (shlahf-tsi-mair) **Schlafzimmer und** look around **das** (tsi-mair) **Zimmer.** Let's learn **die Namen** of the **Dinge in dem Schlafzimmer** just like (vir) **wir** learned the various parts of the **Haus.** Be sure to practice saying **die Wörter** as you (shry-ben) **schreiben** (write) them in the spaces **unten.** Also say out loud the example sentences (oon-tair) **unter den Bildern.**

das (bet) **Bett**

____

Ich kaufe das Bett.

die (bet-deck-ah) **Bettdecke**
blanket

die Bettdecke

Ich (brow-kah) **brauche** (need) **eine Bettdecke.**

das (kohpf-kiss-en) **Kopfkissen**
pillow

____

Das Kopfkissen ist sehr groß.

☐ **der Pfeffer** *(fef-air)*..................	pepper	______________
☐ **das Pfund** *(foont)*....................	pound	______________
☐ **das Photo** *(foh-toh)*..................	photograph	______________
☐ **die Physik** *(fih-zeek)*................	physics	______________
☐ **die Pille** *(pil-ah)*....................	pill	______________

(veck-air)
der Wecker

(kly-dair-shrahnk)
der Kleiderschrank

(nex-sten)
Remove **die nächsten fünf** stickers **und** label these **Dinge** in your **Schlafzimmer.**

(hah-bah)
Ich habe einen Wecker.

(shtayt)
Der Kleiderschrank steht in dem Schlafzimmer.

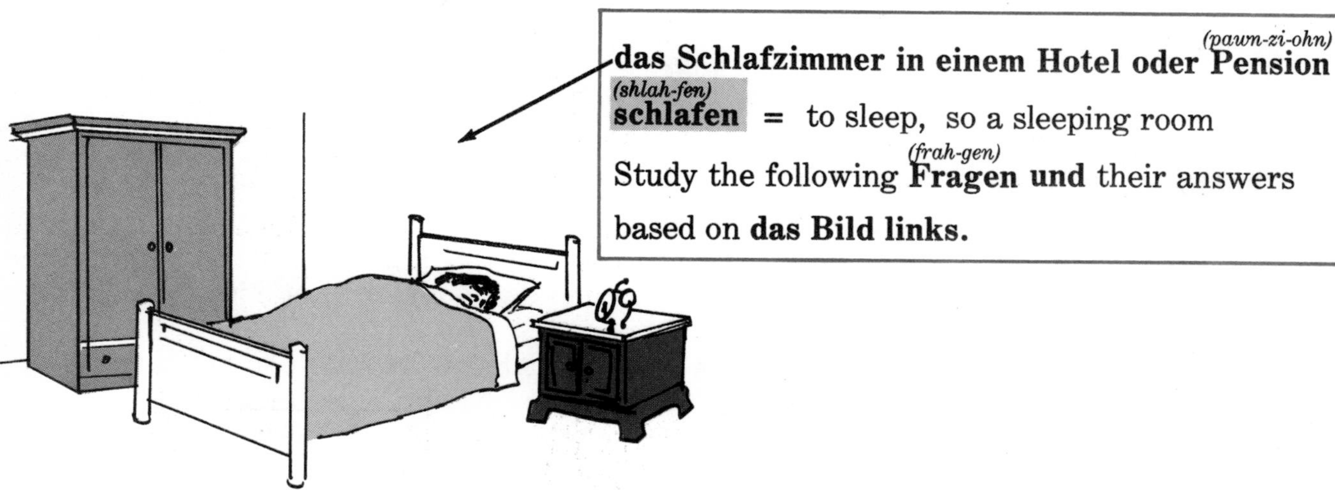

(pawn-zi-ohn)
das Schlafzimmer in einem Hotel oder Pension

(shlah-fen)
schlafen = to sleep, so a sleeping room

(frah-gen)
Study the following **Fragen und** their answers based on **das Bild links.**

1. **Wo ist der Wecker?**
   Der Wecker ist auf dem Tisch.
2. **Wo ist die Bettdecke?**
   Die Bettdecke ist auf dem Bett.
3. **Wo ist der Kleiderschrank?**
   Der Kleiderschrank steht in dem Schlafzimmer.
4. **Wo ist das Kopfkissen?**
   Das Kopfkissen ist auf dem Bett.
5. **Wo ist das Bett?**
   Das Bett steht in dem Schlafzimmer.
6. **Ist das Bett groß oder klein?** *(kline)* small
   Das Bett ist nicht groß.
   Das Bett ist klein.

☐ **das Polen** *(poh-len)*.................. Poland
— **wo sie sprechen Polnisch** *(pohl-nish)*
☐ **die Police** *(poh-lee-sa)*.............. policy
— like an insurance policy
☐ **die Polizei** *(poh-li-tsigh)*............. police

Nun, you answer **die Fragen** based on the previous **Bild.**

Wo ist der Wecker?  **Wo ist das Bett?** 

Der Wecker ist ______________________ ______________________

Let's move into **das Badezimmer und** do the same thing.

(vahsh-beck-en) **das Waschbecken**	(doosh-ah) **die Dusche**	(toy-let-tah) **die Toilette**

das Waschbecken	______________	______________
Das Hotelzimmer hat ein Waschbecken.	**Die Dusche ist nicht in dem Hotelzimmer.**	**Die Toilette ist nicht in dem Hotelzimmer. Die Toilette und die Dusche sind auf der** (eh-tah-zhah) **Etage.** (on the floor)

der (shpee-gel) **Spiegel** (mirror) ______________

das (toohk) **Tuch** (towel) das Tuch

der (vahsh-lah-pen) **Waschlappen** (washcloth) ______________

das (hahnt-toohk) **Handtuch** (hand towel) ______________

das (bah-dah-toohk) **Badetuch** (bath towel) ______________

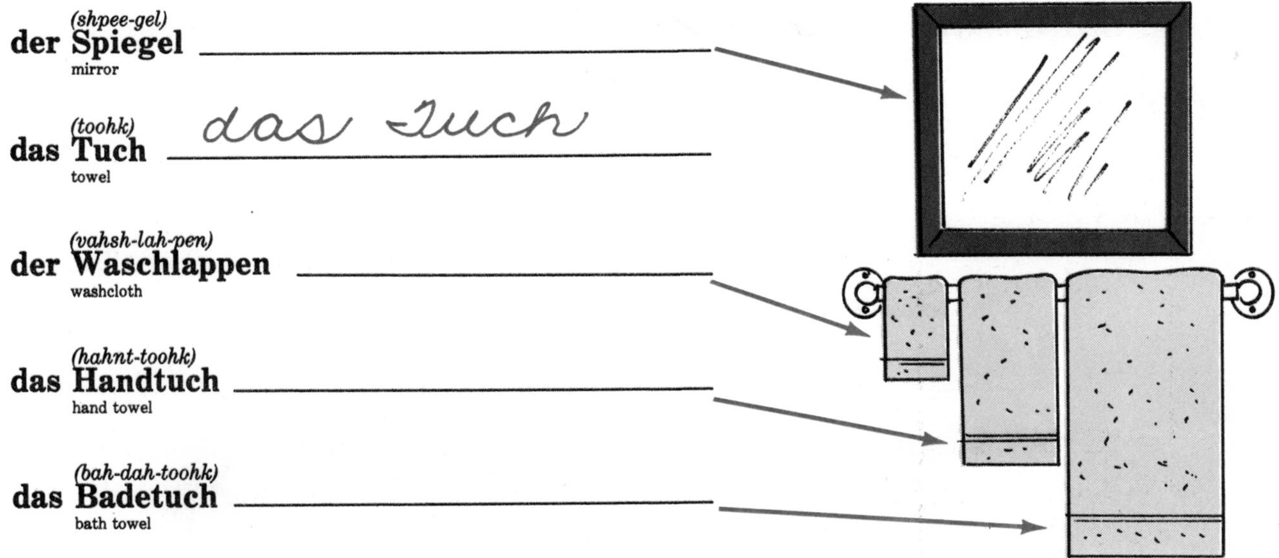

Do not forget to remove **die nächsten sieben** stickers **und** label these **Dinge** in your **Badezimmer.**

☐ **die Politik** *(pohl-li-teek)*..............	politics	______________
☐ **das Portugal** *(pohr-too-gahl)*..........	Portugal	______________
— **wo sie sprechen Portugiesisch** *(pohr-too-gee-zish)*		______________
☐ **die Post** *(post)*.....................	mail	______________
☐ **die Postkarte** *(post-kar-tah)*..........	postcard	______________

das Badezimmer in einem Haus in Europa

baden = to bathe, so a bathing room

Ist die Dusche auf der rechten oder auf der linken Seite in dem Bild? Die Dusche ist auf der ______________ (?) **Seite.**

Wo ist die Toilette *(toy-let-tah)* **oben? Die Toilette ist in der Mitte** *(mit-tah)* (middle)**.**

Wo ist das Waschbecken *(vahsh-beck-en)* **oben? Das Waschbecken ist auf der** ______________ (?) **Seite.**

Wo ist der Spiegel *(shpee-gel)* **oben? Der Spiegel ist über dem** Waschbecken (?)**.**

Wo sind die Badetücher *(bah-dah-tewk-air)* (bath towels) **in dem Bild oben?**

Die Badetücher sind über der ______________ (?)**. Die Badetücher sind an der** ______________ (?)**.**

Remember, **das Badezimmer** *(bah-da-tsi-mair)* means a room **(Zimmer)** to bathe **(baden)** in. If **Sie sind in einem Restaurant und brauchen** *(brow-ken)* the lavatory, **Sie** want to ask for **die Toilette** *not* for **das Badezimmer.**

Restrooms fall **unter** the title of **die Toiletten und sie** are marked **D** **und** **H**. **Sie** will have a sharp surprise if **Sie** think the letters stand **für** "Dudes" **und** "Hers."

D **steht** *(shtayt)* **für Damen** *(dah-men)* (ladies)

und **H** **steht für Herren** *(hair-en)* (men)**.**

☐ **der Priester** *(pree-stair)*.............	priest	______________
☐ **das Problem** *(pro-blame)*.............	problem	______________
☐ **das Programm** *(pro-grahm)*..........	program	______________
☐ **die Qualität** *(kvah-li-tate)*............	quality	______________
☐ **das Restaurant** *(res-tow-rahnt)*.......	restaurant	______________

Next stop — **das Büro,** specifically **der Tisch oder der Schreibtisch** *(shripe-tish)* desk **in dem Büro.** *(bew-roh)* study **Was ist auf** *(owf)* on top of **dem Tisch?** Let's identify **die Dinge** which one normally finds **in dem Büro oder** strewn about **das Haus.**

der Bleistift *(bly-shtift)* pencil

der Kuli *(koo-lee)* pen

der Kuli

das Papier *(pah-peer)*

der Brief *(breef)*

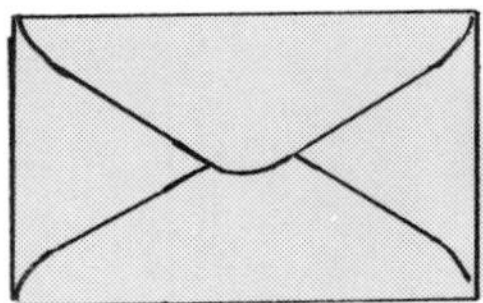

die Postkarte *(post-kar-tah)*

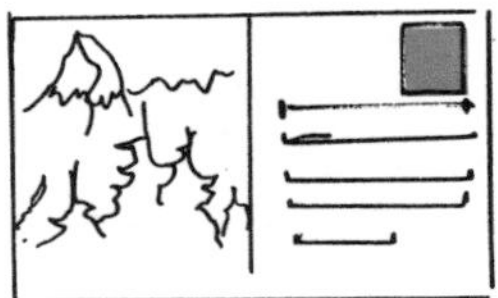

die Briefmarke *(breef-mahr-kah)*

das Buch *(boohk)*

die Zeitschrift *(tsight-shrift)* magazine

die Zeitung *(tsigh-toong)* newspaper

die Brille *(bril-ah)*

der Fernseher *(fairn-zay-air)*

der Papierkorb *(pah-peer-kohrp)*

Hier ist ein sehr gutes <u>nicht</u> freies Wort.

☐ **der Quatsch** *(kvaht-sh)* ______

— This **ist** generally heard in a sentence like **„Das ist Quatsch."** = That is a bunch of baloney.

☐ **das Radio** *(rah-dee-oh)*. . . . . radio ______

☐ **die Religion** *(ray-lee-gee-ohn)*. . . . . religion ______

Nun, label these **Dinge in dem Büro** *(bew-roh)* **mit** your stickers. Do not forget to say these **Wörter** out loud whenever **Sie schreiben** *(shry-ben)* (write) them, **Sie** *(zee)* see them, **oder Sie** apply the stickers. **Nun,** identify **die Dinge in dem Bild unten** by filling in each blank **mit dem richtigen** *(reehk-tee-gen)* (correct) **deutschen Wort** *(vort)*.

1. ____________
2. ____________
3. ____________
4. ____________
5. ____________
6. die Postkarte
7. ____________
8. ____________
9. ____________
10. ____________

Hier sind vier *(fear)* **Verben mehr** *(mair)* (more)**.**

(zeh-en) **sehen** = to see	*(zen-den)* **senden** = to send	*(shlah-fen)* **schlafen** = to sleep	*(fin-den)* **finden** = to find
____________	____________	schlafen	____________

Nun, fill in the blanks, **auf der nächsten** *(nex-sten)* **Seite,** *(zigh-tah)* **mit der richtigen** *(reehk-tee-gen)* form of these **Verben.**

Practice saying the sentences out loud many times.

- ☐ **die Republik** *(ray-poo-bleek)*.......... republic ____________
- ☐ **die Residenz** *(ray-zih-dents)*.......... residence ____________
- ☐ **der Ring** *(ring)*.................... ring ____________
- ☐ **das Risiko** *(ree-zee-koh)*............. risk ____________
- ☐ **rot** *(roht)*......................... red ____________

(zeh-en)
sehen
to see

Ich ______________ **das Bett.**

Er
Sie ______________ **die Bettdecke.**
Es

Wir ______________ **den Wecker.**

Sie (you) ______________ **das Waschbecken.**

Sie (they) sehen **die Dusche.**

(zen-den)
senden
to send

Ich ______________ **den Brief.**

Er
Sie sendet **die Postkarte.**
Es

Wir ______________ **das Buch.**

Sie ______________ **drei Postkarten.**

Sie ______________ **vier Briefe.**

(shlah-fen)
schlafen
to sleep

Ich ______________ **im Schlafzimmer.**

Er
Sie ______________ **im Badezimmer.**
Es

Wir schlafen **im Wohnzimmer.**

Sie ______________ **im Büro.**

Sie ______________ **in der Küche.**

(fin-den)
finden
to find

Ich ______________ **die Briefmarke.**

Er
Sie findet **das Papier.**
Es

Wir ______________ **die Brille.**

Sie ______________ **den Kuli.**

Sie ______________ **die Blumen.**

Remember that **"a"** sounds like "ah." Practice **Land** *(lahnt)*, **schlafen** *(shlah-fen)*, **baden** *(bah-den)*, **danke** *(dahn-kah)*, **was, wann** and **Bank** *(bahnk)*. Also **"au"** is pronounced "ow." Practice **Frau, auf** *(owf)*, **kaufen** *(kow-fen)*, **Haus** *(house)* and **aus** *(ows)*.

Nicht *(neehkt)* means "not" **auf** *(owf)* **Deutsch** *(doych)*. **Nun** *(noon)* practice your pronunciation while **Sie** *(zee)* practice using **"nicht."** Be sure to say the following examples aloud many times.

Das *(dahs)* **ist gut** *(goot)*.
good

Das ist nicht *(neehkt)* **gut.**
not

Heute *(hoy-tah)* **ist Sonntag** *(zohn-tahk)*.
today, Sunday

Heute ist nicht *(neehkt)* **Sonntag.**

Das Auto *(ow-toe)* **ist rot** *(roht)*.
red

Das Auto ist nicht rot.

- ☐ **die Ruine** *(roo-ee-nah)*. . . . . ruins ______________
- ☐ **rund** *(roont)* . . . . round ______________
- ☐ **das Rußland** *(roos-lahnt))*. . . . . Russia ______________
  — wo sie sprechen Russisch *(roo-sish)* ______________
- ☐ **der Salat** *(zah-laht)*. . . . . salad ______________

Step 15

die Post
mail

Sie *(zee)* know **nun** *(noon)* how to count, how to ask **Fragen,** *(frah-gen)* how to use **Verben mit** the "plug-in" formula, how to make statements, **und** how to describe something, be it the location of **a Hotel oder die Farbe** of a **Haus.** Let's now take the basics that **Sie haben** learned **und** expand them in special areas that will be most helpful in your travels. What does everyone do on a holiday? Send postcards, of course. Let's learn exactly how **das deutsche Postamt** *(post-ahmt)* (post office) works.

die Post . . .
nach Amerika
nach Spanien
nach England
nach Italien

Gelb ist die Farbe in Deutschland which identifies **Briefkasten** *(breef-kah-sten)* (mailboxes) **und Telefonzellen** *(tay-lay-fohn-tsel-en)* (telephone booths)**.**
Hier sind the basic **Postamt-Wörter** *(post-ahmt)*. Be sure to practice them out loud **und dann schreiben** *(shry-ben)* **Sie das Wort unter dem Bild.**

der Brief	**die Postkarte**	**die Briefmarke**	**das Telegramm** *(tay-lay-grahm)*
			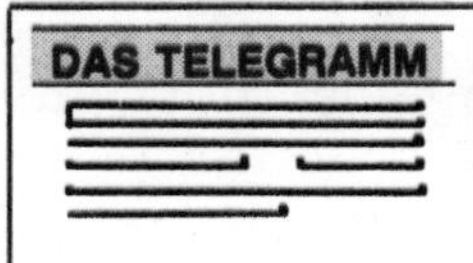
der Brief	________	________	________

- ☐ **das Salz** *(zahlts)*.................... salt ________
- ☐ **sauer** *(zow-air)*.................... sour (vs. sweet = **süß**) ________
- ☐ **scharf** *(sharf)*.................... sharp (spicy) ________
- ☐ **der Scheck** *(sheck)*.................... check ________
- ☐ **das Schiff** *(shiff)*.................... ship ________

(pah-kate)
das Paket

(breef-kah-sten)
der Briefkasten

(looft-post)
mit Luftpost
airmail

(shawl-tair)
der Schalter

(tay-lay-fohn-tsel-ah) *(kah-bee-nah)*
die Telefonzelle/die Kabine

das Telefon

das Telefon

das Postamt

Das deutsche Postamt hat alles *(all-es)* (everything)**. Sie senden** *(zen-den)* (send) **Telegramme** (telegrams)**, Briefe** (letters)**, und Postkarten von** *(fohn)* (from) **dem Postamt. Sie kaufen Briefmarken in dem Postamt. Sie machen Telefonanrufe** *(tay-lay-fohn-on-roo-fah)* (telephone calls) **von dem Postamt.** In large cities, **das Postamt hat einen Schalter** *(shawl-tair)* (counter) which is even **auf** (open) **abends** (evenings) **und am Samstag.** If **Sie** *(zee)* need to call home to **Amerika,** this can be done at **das Postamt und heißt** (is called) **ein Ferngespräch** *(fairn-ge-shprake)* (long-distance call)**.** Okay. First step – **Sie gehen** *(gay-en)* **in das Postamt.**

The following **ist eine gute** *(goo-tah)* sample **Konversation.** Familiarize yourself **mit diesen** *(dee-zen)* (these) **Wörtern nun.** Don't wait until your holiday.

- ☐ **die Schokolade** *(show-koh-lah-dah)*.... chocolate ______
- ☐ **das Schottland** *(shoht-lahnt)*.......... Scotland ______
- ☐ **die Schuhe** *(shoo-ah)*................ shoes ______
- ☐ **die Schule** *(shoo-lah)*................ school ______
- ☐ **die Schweiz** *(shvites)*............... Switzerland ______

Next step — **Sie** ask *(frah-gen)* **Fragen** (questions) like those *(oon-ten)* **unten** depending upon *(vahs)* **was Sie** want.

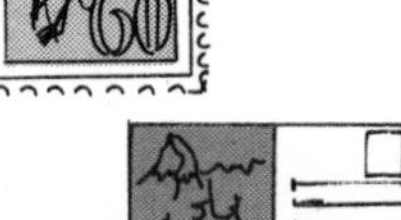

Wo *(voh)* **kaufe** *(kow-fah)* (buy) **ich Briefmarken?**

Wo kaufe ich eine Postkarte?

Wo mache *(mah-kah)* **ich einen Telefonanruf?**

Wo mache ich ein *(fairn-ge-shprake)* **Ferngespräch?**

Wo mache ich ein *(orts-ge-shprake)* **Ortsgespräch?** (local call)

Wo sende *(zen-dah)* **ich ein Telegramm?**

Wo sende ich ein Paket?

Wo ist die Telefonzelle?

(vee-feel) **Wieviel kostet das?**

Wo ist der Postkasten?

Practice these sentences **oben** again and *(vee-dair)* **wieder** (again).

Nun, quiz yourself. See if **Sie** can translate the following thoughts into **Deutsch.**

Die Antworten sind unten auf der *(nex-sten)* **nächsten** (next) **Seite.**

1. Where is a telephone booth? Wo ist eine Telefonzelle? ____________________
2. Where do I make a phone call? ____________________
3. Where do I make a local phone call? ____________________
4. Where do I make a long-distance phone call? ____________________
5. Where is the post office? ____________________

- ☐ **das Schweden** *(shvay-den)*. . . . . Sweden ____________
  — **wo sie sprechen Schwedisch** *(shvay-dish)* ____________
- ☐ **schwimmen** *(shvim-en)* . . . . to swim ____________
- ☐ **die See** *(zay)*. . . . . sea ____________
- ☐ **die Sekunde** *(zay-koon-dah)*. . . . . second ____________

6. Where do I buy stamps? ______________________

7. Airmail stamps? ______________________

8. Where do I send a package? ______________________

9. Where do I send a telegram? ______________________

10. Where is counter eight? ______________________

Hier sind mehr Verben.

(mah-ken) **machen** = to make/do *(tsigh-gen)* **zeigen** = to show *(shry-ben)* **schreiben** = to write *(be-tsah-len)* **bezahlen** = to pay

______________ ______________ schreiben ______________

(mah-ken) **machen** to make/do

Ich ______________ einen *(on-roof)* **Anruf** (call).

Er / Sie / Es ______________ einen Anruf.

Wir machen viel.

Sie (you) ______________ nicht viel.

Sie (they) ______________ alles.

(shry-ben) **schreiben** to write

Ich ______________ einen Brief.

Er / Sie / Es schreibt viel.

Wir ______________ nicht viel.

Sie ______________ *(neehk-ts)* **nichts** (nothing).

Sie ______________ alles.

(tsigh-gen) **zeigen** to show

Ich ______________ *(ee-nen)* **Ihnen** (to you) das Buch.

Er / Sie / Es ______________ Ihnen (to you) das Postamt.

Wir ______________ Ihnen das *(shloh-ss)* **Schloß** (castle).

Sie ______________ mir (to me) das Postamt.

Sie zeigen mir (to me) die Straße.

(be-tsah-len) **bezahlen** to pay

Ich ______________ die *(reck-noong)* **Rechnung** (bill).

Er / Sie / Es ______________ die Theaterkarten.

Wir ______________ die Zugkarten.

Sie bezahlen den Wein.

Sie ______________ die Konzertkarten.

ANTWORTEN

1. Wo ist eine Telefonzelle (Kabine)?
2. Wo mache ich einen Telefonanruf?
3. Wo mache ich ein Ortsgespräch?
4. Wo mache ich ein Ferngespräch?
5. Wo ist das Postamt?
6. Wo kaufe ich Briefmarken?
7. Luftpostbriefmarken?
8. Wo sende ich ein Paket?
9. Wo sende ich ein Telegramm?
10. Wo ist Schalter acht?

Step 16

die Quittung (kvi-toong) [receipt] oder die Rechnung (reck-noong) [bill]

Ja, es gibt (gipt) [there are] **auch** bills to pay **in Deutschland. Sie haben** just finished your evening meal **(Abendessen) und Sie möchten die Rechnung** pay **(bezahlen)**. **Was machen Sie? Sie** call for **den Kellner** (kel-nair) [waiter] **oder die Kellnerin** (kel-nair-in) [waitress]**:**

„Herr Ober!“ (oh-bair) **„Fräulein!“** (froy-line)

Der Kellner will normally reel off what **Sie haben** eaten, while writing rapidly. **Er** will then place **ein kleines** (kline-es) [small] **Stück** (shtewk) [piece] **Papier** (pah-peer) [of paper] **vor** you that looks like **die Rechnung in dem Bild,** while saying something like **„Das macht** (mahkt) [makes] **sechsundzwanzig sechzig.“**

Being a seasoned traveler, **Sie** know that tipping as **wir** know **es in Amerika, ist nicht** a custom **in Deutschland**. Generally **die Bedienung** (be-deen-oong) [service] **ist** included **in den** (dain) **Preisen** (pry-zen) [prices]**.** So, **Sie** pull out **dreißig Mark und,** while placing **das Geld auf den Tisch, Sie sagen,**

Der Kellner then places your **3 DM** change **auf den Tisch und sagt, „Auf Wiedersehen!“**

Sound confusing? **Nein** (nine) [no], just **neu** (noy) [new] **und** different. **Es ist** a custom **in Deutschland,** when paying **in Restaurants,** to round **die Rechnung** (reck-noong) [bill] up to the nearest **Mark oder** half **Mark** according to your preference. So . . .

- ☐ **senden** *(zen-den)* . . . . to send ________
- ☐ **der September** *(zep-tem-bair)* . . . . September ________
- ☐ **sieben** *(zee-ben)* . . . . seven ________
- ☐ **singen** *(zing-en)* . . . . to sing ________
- ☐ **sitzen** *(zit-tsen)* . . . . to sit ________

25,30 DM becomes 25,50 DM **(fünfundzwanzig Mark fünfzig);**

15,17 DM becomes 15,50 DM **(fünfzehn Mark fünfzig);**

15,55 DM becomes 16,00 DM **(sechzehn Mark).**

See how important numbers are!

This simplifies the system of making change **und** avoids a true tipping situation. Watch **die** *(loy-tah)* **Leute** (people) *(oom)* **um** (around) **Sie in einem Restaurant.** At first **es** seems foreign (which **es ist!**), but **Sie** will catch on quickly **und** your familiarity **mit deutschen** customs will be appreciated.

Hier ist a sample *(kohn-fair-zah-tsi-ohn)* **Konversation** involving paying **die** *(reck-noong)* **Rechnung** when leaving a **Hotel.**

Karl:	*(ent-shool-dee-goong)* **Entschuldigung. Ich möchte die** *(reck-noong)* **Rechnung (die Hotelrechnung) bezahlen.**
(hoh-tel-mahn-ah-zhair) Hotelmanager:	*(Vel-ches)* **Welches** (Which) **Zimmer** *(vahr)* **war** (was) **das, bitte?**
Karl:	**Zimmer dreihundertzehn.**
Hotelmanager:	**Danke.** *(ine-in)* **Einen Moment, bitte.**
Hotelmanager:	**Hier ist die** *(reck-noong)* **Rechnung. Das macht neunzig Mark zwanzig.**
Karl:	**Danke (und Karl** hands him **einen Hundertmarkschein. Der Hotelmanager** returns shortly **und sagt)**
Hotelmanager:	**Hier ist** *(ear-ah)* **Ihre** (your) *(kvi-toong)* **Quittung** (bill) **und** *(ear)* **Ihr** (your) **Geld (9,80 DM). Danke schön. Auf Wiedersehen!**

Simple, right? If **Sie** ever **haben** any *(pro-blame-ah)* **Probleme mit Nummern,** just ask the person to write out **die Nummern** so that **Sie** can be sure you understand everything correctly.

Bitte, schreiben (write) **Sie die Nummern** (numbers) **auf!** (out) **Danke.**

Let's take a break from **Geld und,** starting **auf der nächsten Seite,** learn some *(noy-ah)* **neue** (new) fun **Wörter.**

- ☐ **der Ski** *(skee)*...................... ski ____________
- ☐ **die Socken** *(zoh-ken)*................ socks ____________
- ☐ **der Sommer** *(zoh-mair)*.............. summer ____________
- ☐ **die Sonne** *(zoh-nah)*................. sun ____________
- ☐ **die Spezialität** *(shpay-zee-ahl-ih-tate)*.. speciality ____________

Er ist **gesund** *(ge-zoont)*. healthy

Er ist **krank** *(krahnk)*. sick

Das ist **gut** *(goot)*.

Das ist nicht gut.
Das ist **schlecht**.

Das Wasser ist **heiß** *(hice)*.

Es ist 50 Grad.

Das Wasser ist **kalt** *(kahlt)*.

Es ist nur *(noor)* 17 Grad. only

LAUT

leise

Wir sprechen **leise** *(ly-zah)*.

Sie sprechen **laut** *(laut)*.

Die rote Linie ist **kurz** *(koorts)*.

Die blaue Linie ist **lang** *(lang)*.

Die Frau ist **groß**.

Das Kind ist **klein** *(kline)*.

Das rote Buch ist **dick**.

Das grüne Buch ist **dünn** *(dewn)*.

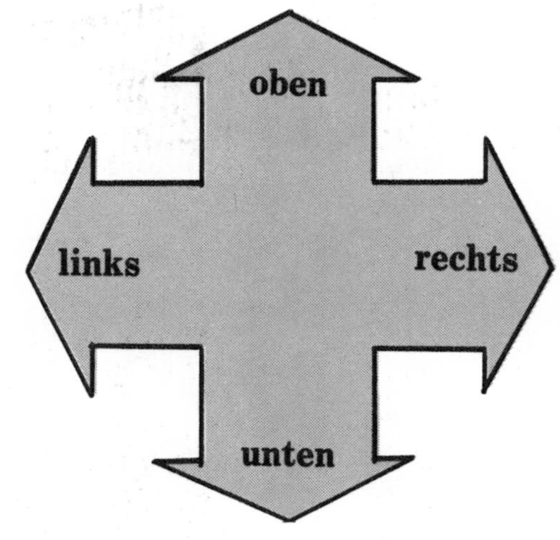

20 Kilometer pro Stunde

200 Kilometer pro Stunde

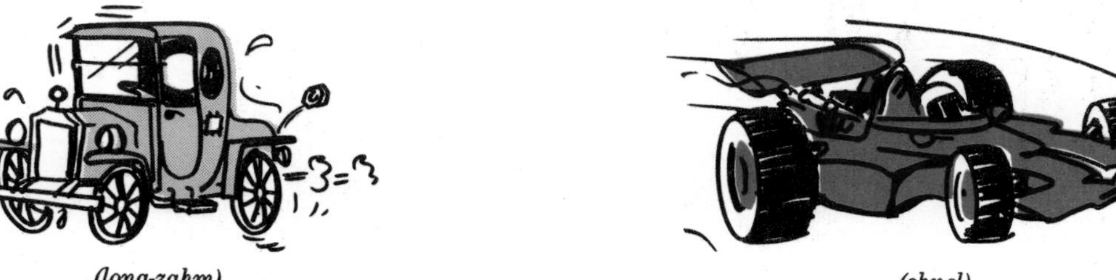

(long-zahm) **langsam** slow

(shnel) **schnell** fast

- ☐ **das Spanien** *(shpah-nee-en)*. . . . . Spain ______
  — wo sie sprechen Spanisch *(shpah-nish)* ______
- ☐ **der Sport** *(shport)*. . . . . sport ______
- ☐ **der Staat** *(shtaht)*. . . . . state/country ______
- ☐ **der Student** *(shtoo-dent)*. . . . . student ______

Die Berge *(bear-gah)* (mountains) sind **hoch** *(hohk)* (high). Sie sind 2000 Meter hoch.

Die Berge sind **niedrig** *(nee-drig)* (low). Sie sind nur 800 Meter hoch.

Der Großvater ist **alt** *(ahlt)* (old). Er ist siebzig Jahre alt.

Das Kind ist **jung** *(yoong)* (young). Es ist nur zehn Jahre alt.

Das Hotelzimmer ist **teuer** *(toy-air)* (expensive). Es kostet 94,50 DM.

Das Pensionzimmer ist **billig** *(bil-ig)* (inexpensive). Es kostet 30,50 DM.

Ich habe 2.000 DM. Ich bin **reich** *(rike)*. Das ist **viel** *(feel)* Geld.

Er hat nur 4 DM. Er ist **arm** *(ahrm)* (poor). Das ist **wenig** *(vay-nig)* (little) Geld.

Hier sind die neuen Verben.

(viss-en) **wissen** = to know (a fact, an address, etc.)	*(kur-nen)* **können** = to be able to, can	*(mew-sen)* **müssen** = to have to, must	*(lay-zen)* **lesen** = to read
______	______	______	lesen

(mew-sen) **Müssen** - *(kur-nen)* **können** - *(viss-en)* **wissen** do not fall neatly into the "plug-in" formula. **Sie sind** actually easier **und sehr** close to **Englisch** in many cases. For **müssen - können - wissen, Sie** only have to learn **zwei** forms for each verb.

(kahn) **kann - können** for **können** *(moos)* **muß - müssen** for **müssen**

(vice) **weiß - wissen** for **wissen**

- ☐ **der Sturm** *(shturm)*.................. storm ______
- ☐ **das Südamerika** *(zewt-ah-mair-ih-kah)*. South America ______
- ☐ **die Suppe** *(zoo-pah)*................. soup ______
- ☐ **die Symphonie** *(zewm-foh-nee)*........ symphony ______
- ☐ **der Tag** *(tahk)*..................... day ______

Study their pattern closely as you will use these *(dry)* **drei Verben** a lot.

(kur-nen)
können
to be able to, can

Ich kann **Deutsch lesen.** (can / German / read)
Er / Sie / Es kann **Deutsch sprechen.**
Wir können **Deutsch verstehen.** (can / understand)
Sie können **Englisch verstehen.** (English / understand)
Sie können **Deutsch lesen.** (read)

(mew-sen)
müssen
to have to, must

Ich muß **die Rechnung bezahlen.** (must / the / bill / pay)
Er / Sie / Es muß **die Rechnung bezahlen.**
Wir müssen **die Hotelrechnung bezahlen.** (must / the / hotel bill / pay)
Sie müssen **die Hotelrechnung bezahlen.**
Sie müssen **die Hotelrechnung bezahlen.**

(viss-en)
wissen
to know

Ich weiß **das.**
Er / Sie / Es weiß **das nicht.**
Wir wissen**, wie alt er ist.**
Sie wissen**, wo das Hotel ist.**
Sie wissen **nichts.** (nothing)

(lay-zen)
lesen
to read

Ich ______ **das Buch.**
Er / Sie / Es ______ **die** *(tsigh-toong)* **Zeitung.**
Wir lesen **das** *(for-moo-lar)* **Formular.** (form)
Sie (you) ______ **wenig.**
Sie (they) ______ **viel.**

Können Sie translate these thoughts **unten** into **Deutsch?** The answers **sind unten.**

1. I can German speak. ______
2. He must now pay. ______
3. We know it not. ______
4. They can the bill pay. ______
5. She knows a lot. Sie weiß viel.
6. I can *(ein bißchen)* a little German speak. ______

ANTWORTEN

1. **Ich kann Deutsch sprechen.**
2. **Er muß nun bezahlen.**
3. **Wir wissen es nicht.**
4. **Sie können die Rechnung bezahlen.**
5. **Sie weiß viel.**
6. **Ich kann ein bißchen Deutsch sprechen.**

Nun, draw **Linien** *(lee-nee-en)* between the opposites **unten.** Don't forget to say them out loud. Use these **Wörter** every day to describe **Dinge in Ihrem** *(ear-em)* [your] **Haus, in der Schule,** *(shoo-lah)* [school] at work, etc.

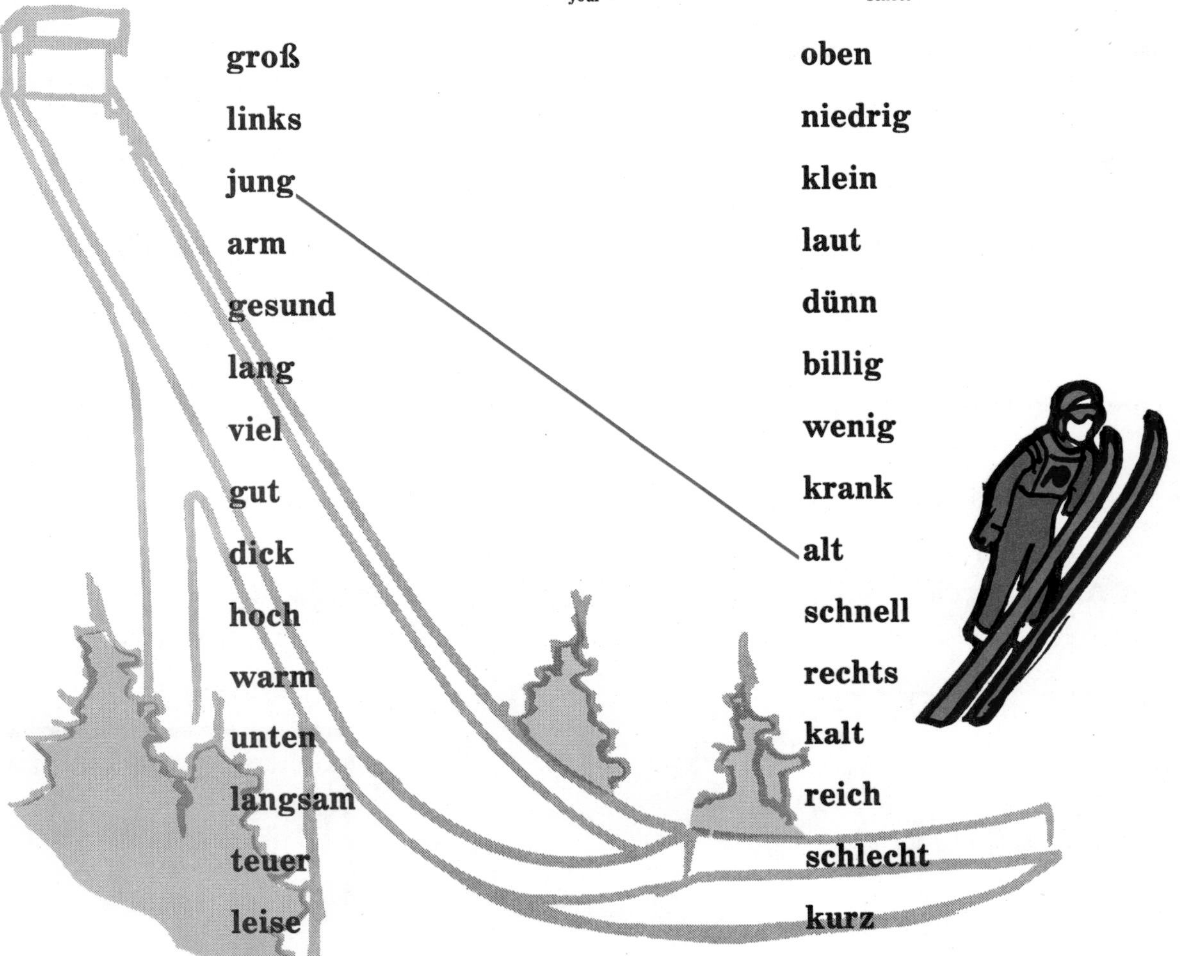

If **Sie** *(zee)* are visiting **Deutschland,** *(doych-lahnt)* **die** *(dee)* **Schweiz** *(shvites)* [Switzerland] **oder Österreich** *(ur-stair-reihk)* [Austria] on a special occasion, **Sie** *(zee)* may want to use one of the following greetings.

Frohe Weihnachten! *(froh-ah) (vie-nahk-ten)* — Merry Christmas

Schönes Neujahr! *(shurn-es) (noy-yahr)* — Happy New Year

Ich gratuliere! *(eehk) (grah-too-lear-ah)* — Congratulations **ODER** **Herzliche Glückswünsche!** *(hairts-leehk-ah) (glewks-veum-shah)* — Congratulations

Alles Gute zum Geburtstag! *(all-es) (goo-tah) (tsoom) (guh-boorts-tahk)* — Happy Birthday

Alles Gute zum Jubiläum! *(you-bih-lay-oom)* — Happy Anniversary

In the following **Wörter**, notice how often **Sie haben ein freies Wort if Sie** change the beginning **T** to a **D.**

- ☐ **der Tanz** *(tahnts)*.................... dance ____________________
- ☐ **tanzen** *(tahn-tsen)* .... to dance ____________________
- ☐ **die Tochter** *(tohk-tair)*.............. daughter ____________________
- ☐ **der Topf** *(tohpf)*..................... pot ____________________

Step 17

(ry-zen) Reisen, *(ry-zen)* Reisen, *(ry-zen)* Reisen
traveling

Gestern nach München! **Heute nach Köln!** **Morgen nach Hamburg!**

Montag in Frankfurt! **Mittwoch in Freiburg!** **Freitag in Nürnberg!**

Traveling **ist** easy, clean, **und sehr** efficient **in Deutschland. Die** *(boon-des-ray-poo-bleek)* **Bundesrepublik Deutschland ist nicht sehr groß. Die Bundesrepublik ist** *(ge-now)* **genau** (exactly) *(zoh)* **so** (as) **groß** *(vee)* **wie** (as) **Oregon oder Kolorado und das macht das Reisen sehr** *(ine-fahk)* **einfach** (simple)**. Wie reisen Sie** *(durhk)* **durch** (through) **Deutschland?**

Hans *(ry-st)* **reist** (travels) **mit** *(daim)* **dem Auto.** 

Anita reist mit dem Zug. 

Helene reist mit dem Flugzeug. 

Hermine reist mit dem Schiff.

Karl und Annette reisen mit dem Fahrrad durch Deutschland. 

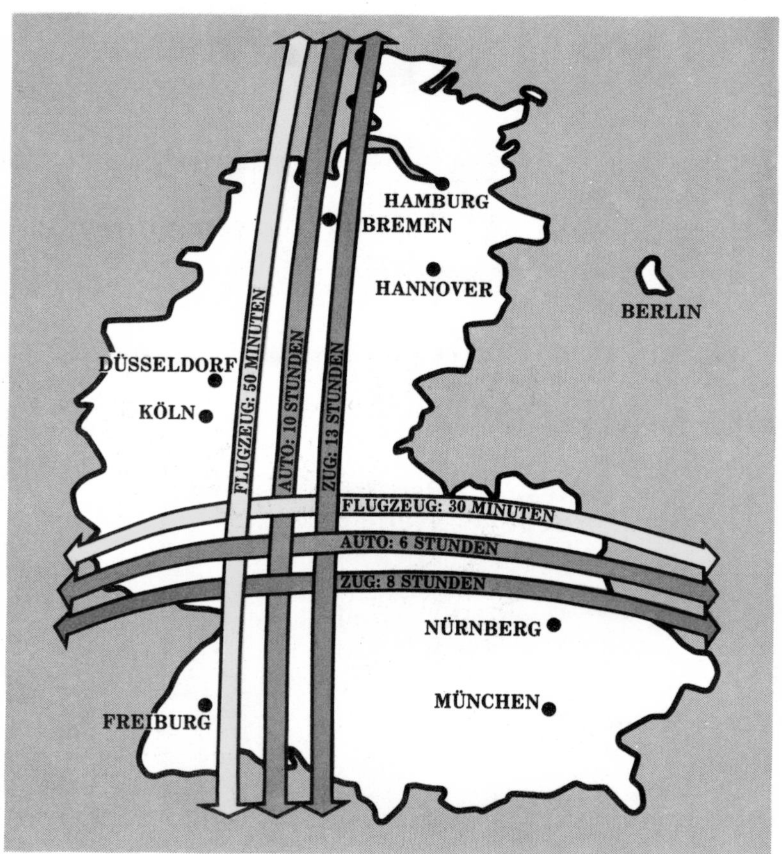

Sehen Sie die Landkarte links? Das ist die Bundesrepublik. Es *(dow-airt)* **dauert** (takes) **nur 50 Minuten von Nord nach Süd mit dem Flugzeug, 10 Stunden mit dem Auto, und 13 Stunden mit dem Zug. Gut, nicht** *(vahr)* **wahr?** (isn't it) **Ja!**

- ☐ **träumen** *(troy-men)* . . . . to dream
- ☐ **trinken** *(trink-en)* . . . . to drink
- ☐ **tun** *(toon)* . . . . to do
- ☐ **die Tür** *(tewr)* . . . . door
- ☐ **die Uniform** *(oo-nee-form)* . . . . uniform

Die deutschen Leute (loy-tah) [people] love to travel, so **es ist** no surprise to find many **Wörter** built on the **Wort „Reisen"** which can mean either "trip" **oder** "travel." Practice saying the following **Wörter** many times. **Sie** will see them **oft.**

Unten sind some basic signs which **Sie** should **auch** learn to recognize quickly. **Gang** (gong) comes from the verb **gehen** meaning "to go" **oder** "to walk." That should help you **mit diesen** (dee-zen) [these] **Wörtern.**

Eingang

AUSGANG

der Haupteingang *(howpt-ine-gong)* main entrance ____________

kein Eingang *(kine) (ine-gong)* no entrance ____________

der Eingang *(ine-gong)* entrance der Eingang

der Ausgang *(ows-gong)* exit ____________

der Notausgang *(note-ows-gong)* emergency exit ____________

der Hauptausgang *(howpt-ows-gong)* main exit ____________

kein Ausgang *(ows-gong)* no exit ____________

- ☐ **das Ungarn** *(oon-garn)*.............. Hungary ____________
  — wo sie sprechen Ungarisch *(oon-gar-ish)* ____________
- ☐ **uninteressant** *(oon-in-tair-es-sahnt)* .... uninteresting ____________
- ☐ **die Universität** *(oo-ni-vair-zi-tate)*..... university ____________
- ☐ **der Untergrund** *(oon-tair-groont)*..... underground (subway) ____________

(fahr)
Fahr, on the other hand, comes from the verb **fahren** which means "to go by vehicle" **oder** "to drive." These **sind** signs that **Sie** will see on the *(ow-toh-bahn)* **Autobahn,** (freeway) plus . . .

(ine-fahrt) **die Einfahrt** (entrance for a vehicle) ____________________

(ows-fahrt) **die Ausfahrt** (exit for a vehicle) die Ausfahrt

die Fahrkarte (ticket) ____________________

Gute Fahrt! (trip) ____________________

Hier sind vier sehr *(veehk-tee-guh)* **wichtige** opposites.

Von Frankfurt nach

München und zurück

Ffm ab	ZugNr	an	Bemerkungen	ab	ZugNr	Ffman	Bemerkungen
0.15	D 52	6.05	U Würzburg	© 1.20	E 608	8.16	U Stuttg D ♀ oG
1.44	D 364	7.04	🛏 ▬ ♀	6.44	E 783	12.04	(Sa u † oG)
3.30	D 308	8.46	🚃 ♀ (abWürzbg)				U Würzburg
7.04	D 30	11.50	✕	7.06	D 465	12.09	⊠
Ⓑ 7.05	F♦ 120	10.48	🚋 ✕	7.24	TEE 11	11.56	✕ ◇ ☎ U
7.10	D 312	11.58	🚋 ✕ U Nürnb E				Mannh ✕ ◇ ☎
7.23	E 658	12.15	🚃 ab Würzb D ♀	7.52	D 81	12.13	✕ U Würzb ✕
8.12	D 245	13.10	✕	8.30	F♦ 33	12.32	✕ ◇ ☎
8.33	E 692	14.51	U Nürnberg	8.50	D 427	13.34	✕
8.44	N2628	13.57	U Mhm F♦ ✕ ◇ ☎	Ⓑ 10.30	D 460	15.12	♀ U Stuttgart ✕
Sa 9.21	D2530	14.45	oG ♀	11.11	D 267	16.17	✕ U Heidelbg E ♀
9.38	D 530	14.53	✕	12.28	D 83	16.57	✕ U Würzburg ⊠
© 9.47	F♦ 38	13.44	✕	12.50	D 257	18.21	♀
9.55	D 258	14.58	♀	13.04	TEE 21	17.02	✕ ◇ ☎
10.00	E 560	15.16	U Heidelberg D ✕	13.10	D 481	18.00	♀ U Nürnberg ✕
Ⓐ 10.39	D1314	15.16	⊠	Fr 13.51	D2529	18.56	oG ♀
11.01	D 304	15.03	✕ U Würzburg	13.58	D 529	19.10	✕
			TEE ✕ ◇ ☎	14.35	D 383	19.46	✕ U Würzb E
11.01	D 304	16.04	✕ U Würzbg ✕	14.45	D 403	20.00	✕ U Heidelb ✕ oG

(on-koonft) **die Ankunft** (arrival) ____________________

(ahp-fahrt) **die Abfahrt** (departure) ____________________

(ows-lahnt) **ausland** (foreign) ausland

(in-lahnt) **inland** (domestic) ____________________

Let's learn the basic travel **Verben.** Follow the same pattern **Sie haben** in previous Steps.

(fahr-en) **fahren** = to drive/travel by vehicle ____________________

(flee-gen) **fliegen** = to fly ____________________

(zit-zen) **sitzen** = to sit ____________________

(booh-ken) **buchen** = to book, as in reserve ____________________

(lahn-den) **landen** = to land landen

(on-koh-men) **ankommen** = to arrive ____________________

(ahp-fahr-en) **abfahren** = to depart ____________________

(shtai-gen) **steigen** = to climb ____________________

(oom-shtai-gen) **umsteigen** = to transfer ____________________

einsteigen = to climb into/board ____________________

aussteigen = to get out/disembark ____________________

- ☐ **unten** *(oon-ten)* . . . . downstairs ____________________
- ☐ **unter** *(oon-tair)* . . . . under ____________________
- ☐ **voll** *(fohl)* . . . . full ____________________
  — ex. **Das Glas ist voll.**
  Der Mann ist voll *(drunk)*.

Mit diesen Verben, Sie sind ready for any **Reise** anywhere. Using the "plug-in" formula for **Verben** which **Sie haben** drilled previously, translate the following thoughts into **Deutsch.** The answers **sind unten.**

1. I fly to Frankfurt. Ich fliege nach Frankfurt
2. I drive to Bonn. ____________________
3. We land in Hamburg. ____________________
4. He sits in the airplane. ____________________
5. She books the trip to America. ____________________
6. They travel to Berlin. ____________________
7. Where is the train to Salzburg? ____________________
8. How fly I to England? With Pan Am or with Lufthansa? ____________________

____

Hier sind mehr neue Wörter für die Reise. As always, write out **die Wörter und** practice the sample sentences out loud.

(bahn-hohf)
der Bahnhof
train station

der Bahnhof

Entschuldigung. Wo ist der Bahnhof?

(howpt-bahn-hohf)
der Hauptbahnhof = Hbf
main train station

____

Entschuldigung. Wo ist der Hauptbahnhof?

(flook-hah-fen)
der Flughafen
airport

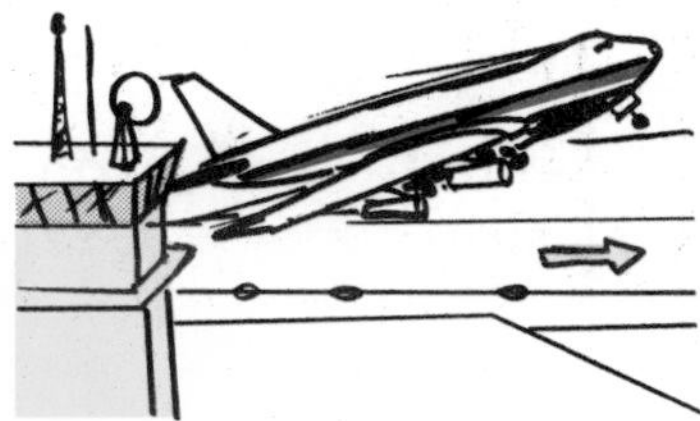

____

Entschuldigung. Wo ist der Flughafen?

ANTWORTEN

1. **Ich fliege nach Frankfurt.**
2. **Ich fahre nach Bonn.**
3. **Wir landen in Hamburg.**
4. **Er sitzt in dem Flugzeug.**
5. **Sie bucht die Reise nach Amerika.**
6. **Sie reisen nach Berlin.**
7. **Wo ist der Zug nach Salzburg?**
8. **Wie fliege ich nach England? Mit Pan Am oder mit Lufthansa?**

(veck-sel-shtoo-bah)
die Wechselstube
money-exchange office

____

Entschuldigung. Wo ist die Wechselstube?

(foont-bew-roh)
das Fundbüro
lost-and-found office

____

Entschuldigung. Wo ist das Fundbüro?

(fahr-plahn)
der Fahrplan
timetable/schedule

der Fahrplan

Entschuldigung. Wo ist der Fahrplan?

(be-zetst)
besetzt ______________________
occupied

(ahp-tile)
das Abteil das Abteil
compartment

(plahts)
der Platz ______________________
seat

Ist dieser Platz besetzt? ______________________

Ist dieses Abteil besetzt? ______________________

Practice writing out the following *(frah-gen)* **Fragen.** **Es** will help you *(shpay-tair)* **später** (later).

Bitte, wo ist die Toilette? ______________________

Bitte, wo ist Abteil neun? ______________________

Wo ist der *(vahr-tah-zahl)* **Wartesaal?** (waiting room) Wo ist der Wartesaal?

Wo ist Schalter acht? ______________________

Ist *(rau-ken)* **Rauchen** (smoking) *(fair-boh-ten)* **verboten** (prohibited)**?** ______________________

- ☐ **von** *(fohn)* .... from
  - — ex. **Der Zug kommt von Berlin.**
  - **Die Frau kommt von Gießen.**
- ☐ **vor** *(for)* .... before/in front of
  - — ex. **Das Kind steht vor dem Hotel.**

Increase your travel **Wörter** by writing out **die Wörter unten und** practicing the sample sentences out loud.

(nahk)
nach ______________________
to
Wo ist der Zug nach Paris?

(tsight)
Zeit ______________________
time
Ich habe wenig Zeit.

(glice)
das Gleis ______________________
track
Der Zug fährt vom Gleis 7 ab.

(bahn-shtike)
der Bahnsteig der Bahnsteig
platform
Der Zug kommt auf Bahnsteig 8 an.

Practice these **Wörter** every day. **Sie** will be surprised **wie oft Sie** will use them. **Können Sie** the following *(lay-zen)* **lesen?** read

Sie sitzen nun im Flugzeug und Sie *(flee-gen)* **fliegen nach Deutschland. Sie haben Geld** exchanged (you have, haven't you?), **Sie haben die Fahrkarten und den Paß, und Sie haben den Reisekoffer** packed. **Sie sind nun Tourist. Sie** *(lahn-den)* **landen morgen um 14:15 in Deutschland. Gute Reise!** *(feel)* **Viel** *(shpahss)* **Spaß!**

Nun, Sie have arrived **und Sie** head for the *(bahn-hohf)* **Bahnhof** in order to get to your final destination. **Deutsche** *(tsew-gah)* **Züge** (trains) come in many shapes, sizes, **und** speeds. **Es** *(gipt)* **gibt** (there are) *(pair-zoh-nen-tsew-gah)* **Personenzüge (sehr langsam),** *(ile-tsew-gah)* **Eilzüge (langsam),** *(shnel-tsew-gah)* **Schnellzüge (schnell), und** *(in-tair)* **Inter-City** *(tsew-gah)* **Züge (sehr schnell).** Some **Züge haben einen** *(shpy-zah-vah-gen)* **Speisewagen** (dining car) **und some Züge haben einen Schlafwagen** (sleeping car) **oder einen** *(lee-gah-vah-gen)* **Liegewagen** (car with berths)**.** All this will be indicated on the **Zugfahrplan,** but remember, **Sie wissen auch** how to ask **Dinge** like this. Practice your possible **Frage** combinations by writing out the following samples.

Hat der Zug einen *(shpy-zah-vah-gen)* **Speisewagen?** Hat der Zug einen Speisewagen?

Hat der Zug einen *(lee-gah-vah-gen)* **Liegewagen?** ______________________

Hat der Zug einen *(shlahf-vah-gen)* **Schlafwagen?** ______________________

- ☐ **das Volk** *(folk)*.................... folk/people ______________________
- ☐ **der Vater** *(fah-tair)*................ father ______________________
  — ex. **Der Vater heißt Herr Taler.** ______________________
- ☐ **der Vorname** *(for-nah-mah)*.......... first name ______________________
  — ex. **Der Vater heißt Helmut mit Vorname.** ______________________

What about inquiring about **Preisen?** **Sie** *(kur-nen)* **können das auch fragen.**

(vahs) **Was** **kostet** *(dee)* **die Fahrt nach** *(high-del-bairg)* **Heidelberg?** ____________________

(ine-fahk) **einfach** (one-way) einfach ____________________ **hin und** *(tsoo-rewk)* **zurück** (there and back (round-trip)) ____________________

Was kostet die Fahrt nach *(veen)* **Wien?** (Vienna) ____________________

Was kostet die Fahrt nach *(koh-pen-hah-gen)* **Kopenhagen?** ____________________

Einfach oder hin und zurück? ____________________

What about *(ahp-fahrt)* **Abfahrt** (departure) **und** *(on-koonft)* **Ankunft** (arrival) times? **Sie** *(kur-nen)* **können das auch fragen!**

(vahn) **Wann** *(gate)* **geht der Zug nach** *(mahr-burg)* **Marburg?** Wann geht der Zug nach Marburg?

Wann geht der *(flook)* **Flug nach** *(rohm)* **Rom?** ____________________

Wann kommt der *(tsook)* **Zug aus** *(mah-drid)* **Madrid?** ____________________

Wann kommt der Flug aus *(bear-leen)* **Berlin?** ____________________

Sie have arrived **in Deutschland. Sie sind nun** *(ahm)* **am** (at the) **Bahnhof. Wo** do **Sie** want to go? Well, tell that to the person at the **Schalter** selling **Karten!**

Ich *(murk-tah)* **möchte nach** *(dort-moont)* **Dortmund fahren.** (to travel) ____________________

Ich möchte nach *(lew-beck)* **Lübeck fahren.** ____________________

Wir möchten nach Innsbruck fahren. ____________________

(vahn) **Wann geht der Zug nach Innsbruck?** ____________________

(vahs) **Was kostet eine Karte nach Innsbruck?** ____________________

Ich möchte eine Karte nach Innsbruck. ____________________

(air-sta) **erste** (first) *(klah-sah)* **Klasse** (class) erste Klasse ____________________ *(tsvai-tah)* **zweite** (second) *(klah-sah)* **Klasse** (class) ____________________

Einfach oder hin und zurück? ____________________

(moos) **Muß ich** *(oom-shtai-gen)* **umsteigen?** ____________________ *(dahn-kah)* **Danke.** ____________________

Mit this practice, **Sie sind** off **und** running. **Diese Reisewörter** will make your holiday twice as enjoyable **und** at least three times as easy. Review **diese neuen Wörter** by doing the crossword puzzle **auf Seite** 77. Practice drilling yourself on this Step by selecting other locations **und** asking your own **Fragen** about **Züge, Busse** *(boos-sah)*, **oder Flugzeuge** *(flook-tsoy-gah)* that go there. Select **neue Wörter** from your **Wörterbuch und** practice asking questions that

beginnen mit **WO** **WANN** **WAS KOSTET** **WIE OFT**

oder making statements like **Ich möchte nach Hamburg fahren. Ich möchte eine Karte kaufen.**

ACROSS

1. restaurant
2. to drive, go to
3. train
4. money
5. sleeping car
6. entrance
7. free, available
8. nothing
9. I
10. yes
11. exit (for cars)
12. exit (for people)
13. to fly
14. ticket
15. trip
16. no
17. train trip

DOWN

1. smoker
2. airport
10. yes
19. time
20. suitcase
21. simple/one way
22. travel info
23. to
24. with
25. train station
26. foreign
27. non-smoker
28. passport
29. ocean voyage
30. occupied
31. she
32. he
33. domestic

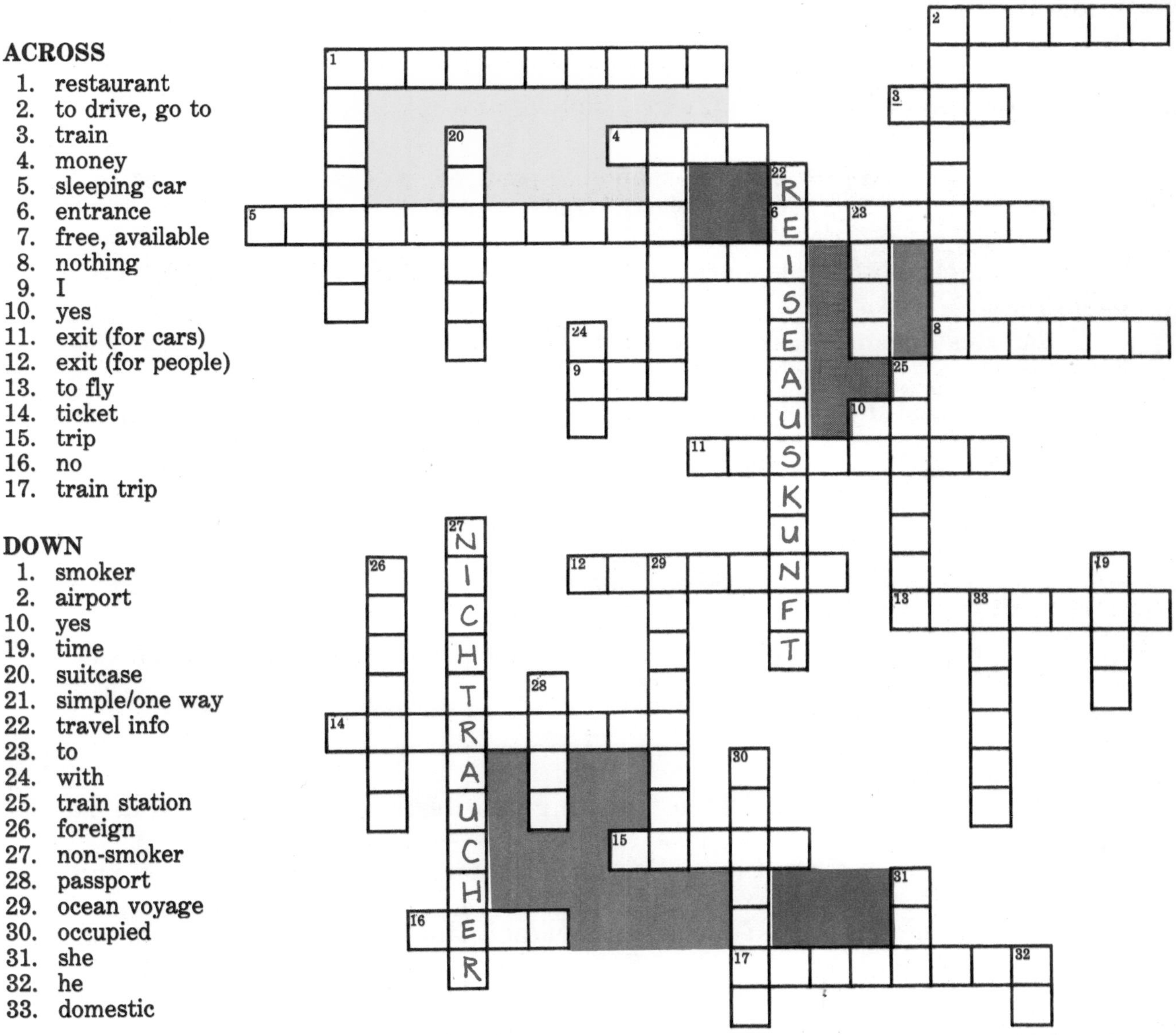

ANTWORTEN ZUM KREUZWORTRÄTSEL

ACROSS

1. **Restaurant**
2. **fahren**
3. **Zug**
4. **Geld**
5. **Schlafwagen**
6. **Eingang**
7. **frei**
8. **nichts**
9. **ich**
10. **ja**
11. **Ausfahrt**
12. **Ausgang**
13. **fliegen**
14. **Fahrkarte**
15. **Reise**
16. **nein**
17. **Zugreise**

DOWN

1. **Raucher**
2. **Flughafen**
10. **ja**
19. **Zeit**
20. **Koffer**
21. **einfach**
22. **Reiseauskunft**
23. **nach**
24. **mit**
25. **Bahnhof**
26. **ausland**
27. **Nichtraucher**
28. **Pass**
29. **Seereise**
30. **besetzt**
31. **sie**
32. **er**
33. **inland**

Step 18

Sie sind nun in Deutschland und Sie haben ein Hotelzimmer. Und nun? Sie sind hungrig *(hoon-grig)* (hungry)**.** **Sie möchten essen. Wo ist ein gutes** *(goo-tes)* **Restaurant?** First of all, **es gibt** *(gipt)* (there are) different types of places to eat. Let's learn them.

das Gasthaus *(gahst-house)* **/ der Gasthof** *(gahst-hohf)*	= an inn with a full range of meals
das Café *(kah-fay)*	= a coffee shop with pastries, snacks **und** beverages (This should be a regular stop every day about 3:30 p.m.)
der Schnellimbiß *(shnel-im-biss)*	= a snack bar, usually specializing in **Wurst** *(vurst)* (sausages) **und** beverages
das Restaurant	= exactly what it says, with a variety of meals
die Weinstube *(vine-shtoo-bah)*	= a small, cozy restaurant specializing in **Weine** with some hot dishes, cheeses, **und** snacks
die Bierhalle *(beer-hahl-ah)*	= besides **Bier, Sie können auch** hot dishes, **Wurst**, pretzels **und Salate** *(zah-lah-tah)* **bestellen**
der Ratskeller *(rahts-kel-lair)*	= a type of restaurant frequently found in the basement of **das Rathaus** *(raht-house)* (city hall)

Try all of them. Experiment. **Sie finden nun ein gutes Restaurant. Sie gehen in das Restaurant und Sie finden einen Platz** *(plahts)*. Sharing **Tische** (tables) **mit** others **ist** a common **und sehr** pleasant custom **in Europa.** If **Sie sehen** *(zay-en)* a vacant **Stuhl** *(shtool)*, just be sure to first ask

Entschuldigung *(ent-shool-dee-goong)*. **Ist dieser Platz frei** *(fry)*?

If **Sie brauchen** *(brow-ken)* (need) **eine Speisekarte**, catch the attention of the **Kellner und** say

Herr Ober! Die Speisekarte, bitte.

☐ **die Vereinigten Staaten** *(fair-eye-neehk-ten shtah-ten)*. . United States ______

— ex. **Ich wohne in den Vereinigten Staaten.** ______
Ich komme aus den Vereinigten Staaten. ______
Ich arbeite in den Vereinigten Staaten. ______
Ich reise in den Vereinigten Staaten. ______

In Deutschland, es gibt drei main meals to enjoy every day, plus **Kaffee** *(kah-fay)* **und Kuchen** *(koo-khen)* (pastry) in the **späten Nachmittag.**

das Frühstück *(frew-shtewk)*	= breakfast	**in Hotels und Pensionen** *(pawn-tsi-oh-nen)* this meal may start as early as 6:00 **und** finish at 8:00. Be sure to check the schedule before you retire for the night.
das Mittagessen *(mit-tahk-es-sen)* (midday meal)	= lunch	generally served from 11:30 to 14:00. For most people, this **ist** the main meal of the day.
das Abendessen *(ah-bent-es-sen)*	= dinner	generally served from 18:00 to 20:30 and sometimes later; frequently after 21:30, only cold snacks **oder heiße** (hot) **Wurst** are served in **Restaurants**.

If **Sie** look around you **in einem Restaurant, Sie** will see that some **deutsche Tisch** customs **sind** different from ours. For example, **Kartoffeln sind** never cut **mit einem Messer**. Before starting **das Essen, Sie** always wish **die Leute** in your party **oder** those sharing your **Tisch** **„Guten Appetit."** Before clearing the dishes, **der Kellner** will ask, **„Hat's geschmeckt?"** **Er** is asking if **Sie** enjoyed your **Essen und** if it tasted good. A smile **und** a **„Ja, danke"** will tell him that you enjoyed it.

Nun, it may be **Frühstück** *(frew-shtewk)* time **in Denver**, but **Sie sind in Deutschland und es ist 18 Uhr**. Most **deutsche Restaurants** post **die Speisekarte** outside. Always read it before entering so **Sie wissen** *(viss-en)* what type of meals **und Preisen** *(pry-zen)* (prices) **Sie** will encounter inside. Most **Restaurants** offer **ein Menü** *(men-ew)* **oder ein Tagesgericht** *(tah-ges-ge-reehkt)* (special meal of the day). This is a complete meal at a fair **Preis** *(price)*. In addition, **es gibt** all the following main categories **auf der Speisekarte.**

- ☐ **das Wasser** *(vah-sair)*.............. water ______________
- ☐ **der Westen** *(ves-ten)*.............. West ______________
- ☐ **das Wild** *(vilt)*..................... venison ______________
- ☐ **der Wein** *(vine)*..................... wine ______________
- ☐ **der Wind** *(vint)*..................... wind ______________

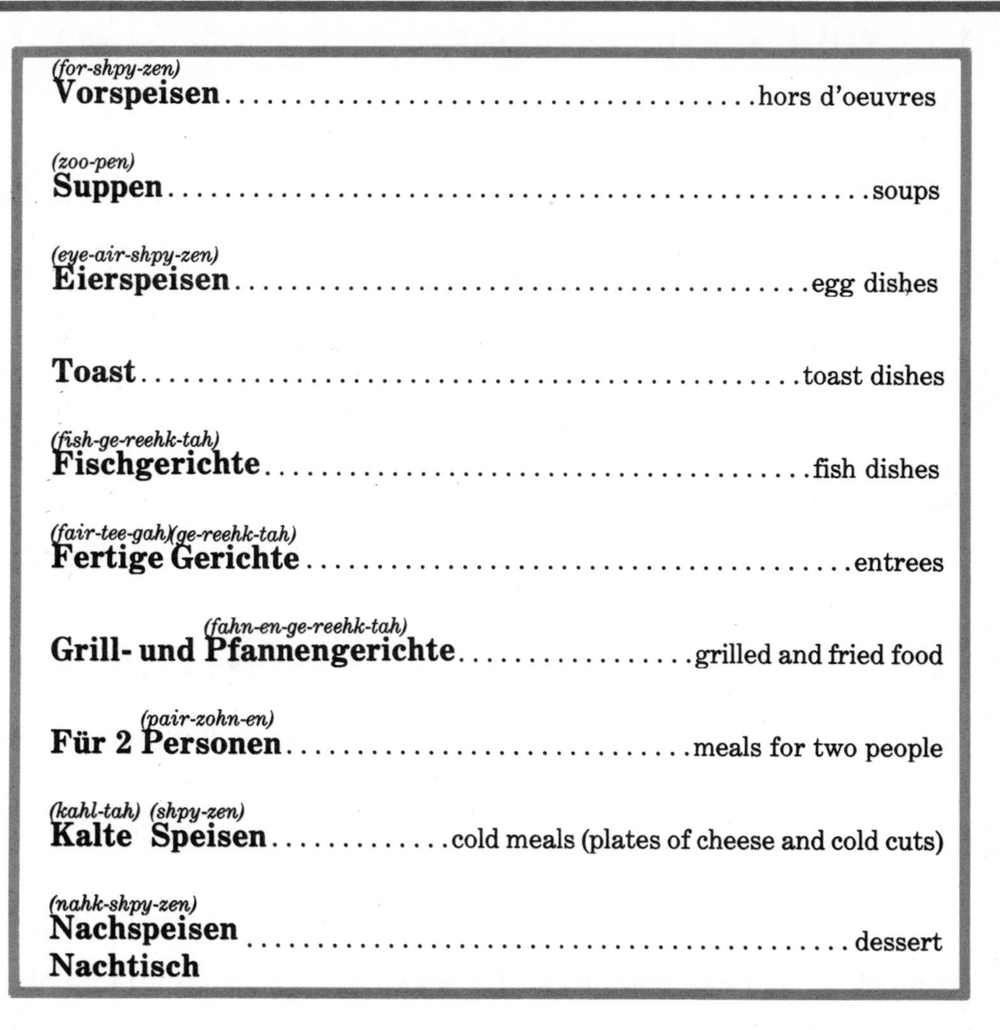

(for-shpy-zen)
Vorspeisen .... hors d'oeuvres

(zoo-pen)
Suppen .... soups

(eye-air-shpy-zen)
Eierspeisen .... egg dishes

Toast .... toast dishes

(fish-ge-reehk-tah)
Fischgerichte .... fish dishes

(fair-tee-gah)(ge-reehk-tah)
Fertige Gerichte .... entrees

(fahn-en-ge-reehk-tah)
Grill- und Pfannengerichte .... grilled and fried food

(pair-zohn-en)
Für 2 Personen .... meals for two people

(kahl-tah) (shpy-zen)
Kalte Speisen .... cold meals (plates of cheese and cold cuts)

(nahk-shpy-zen)
Nachspeisen
Nachtisch .... dessert

Most **Restaurants** also offer **Spezialitäten** *(shpay-tsee-ahl-ih-tate-en)* [specialties] **des Hauses oder** specific meals prepared **nach Art des Hauses** [according to the chef's style]. If **Sie** happen to be traveling **mit Kindern**, look for the **Kinderteller** *(kin-dair-tell-air)* [children's plate]. **Nun** for a preview of delights to come . . . At the back of this **Buch Sie finden eine** sample **deutsche Speisekarte. Lesen** *(lay-zen)* [read] **Sie die Speisekarte heute und lernen Sie die neuen Wörter!** When **Sie** are ready to leave for **Europa** *(oy-roh-pah)*, cut out **die Speisekarte** *(shpy-zah-kar-tah)*, fold it **und** carry it in your pocket, wallet, **oder** purse. **Sie** can **nun** go in any **Restaurant und** feel prepared! (May I suggest studying **die Speisekarte** before **und** not after **Sie haben** eaten!)

☐ **der Winter** *(vin-tair)*	winter	____________
☐ **die Wolle** *(voh-lah)*	wool	____________
☐ **Willkommen!** *(vill-koh-men)*	Welcome!	____________
☐ **wandern** *(vahn-dairn)*	to wander	____________
☐ **die Waren** *(vahr-en)*	wares	____________

In addition, learning the following should help you to identify what kind of meat **oder** poultry **Sie bestellen** (order) **und** *(vee)* **wie es** will be prepared.

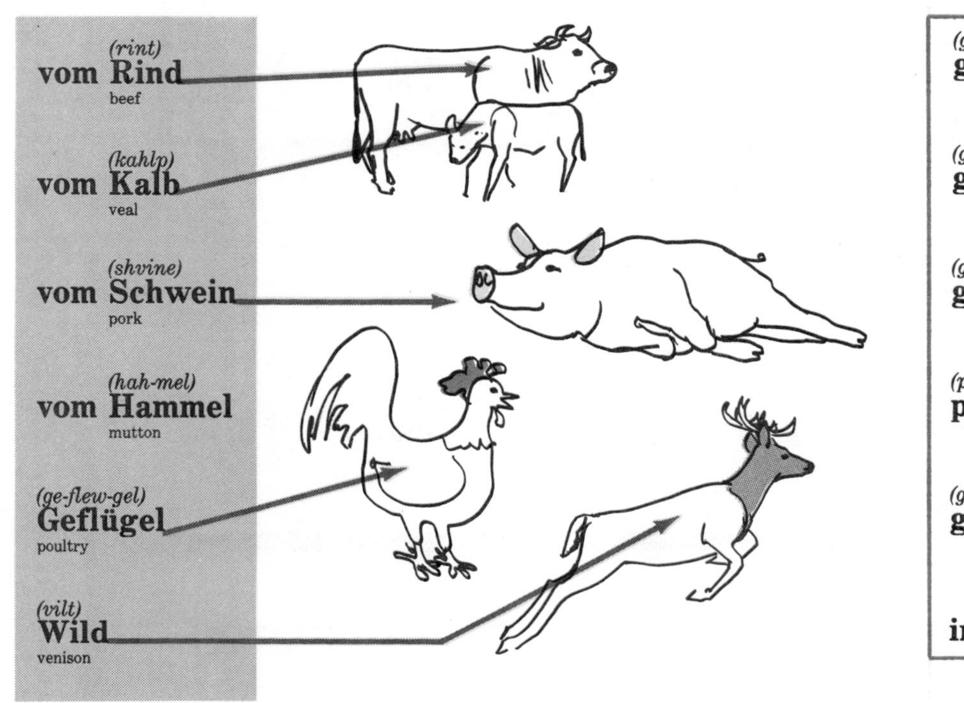

(ge-kohkt) **gekocht** = cooked

(ge-brah-ten) **gebraten** = roasted/fried

(ge-bah-ken) **gebacken** = baked

(pahn-ear-t) **paniert** = breaded

(ge-grilt) **gegrillt** = grilled

(bahk-taig) **im Backteig** = in batter

Sie will also get *(ge-mew-zah)* **Gemüse** (vegetables) **und** *(kahr-toh-feln)* **Kartoffeln** (potatoes) **mit** your **Essen und einen** *(ge-mish-ten)* **gemischten** (mixed) **Salat.** One day at an open-air **Markt** (market) will teach you **die Namen** for all the different kinds of **Gemüse und** *(ohpst)* **Obst,** (fruit) plus it will be a delightful experience for you. **Sie können** always consult your menu guide at the back of this **Buch** if **Sie** *(fair-gess-en)* **vergessen** (forget) **den richtigen Namen. Nun Sie haben** decided **was Sie möchten essen und der Kellner kommt.**

- ☐ **warm** *(varm)* . . . . warm __________
- ☐ **die Warnung** *(vahr-noong)* . . . . warning __________
- ☐ **wünschen** *(vewn-shen)* . . . . to wish __________
  — ex. **Was wünschen Sie?** __________
- ☐ **der Weg** *(veg)* . . . . way __________

Don't forget about treating yourself to a **Nachtisch oder Nachspeise**. You would **nicht** want to miss out on trying the following desserts.

(ge-mish-tes) (ice)
Gemischtes Eis
two or three scoops of ice cream

(ice-beck-air) (frewk-ten)
Eisbecher mit Früchten
an ice-cream cup **mit** fruit, liqueur **und** whipped cream

(zah-nah)
Gemischtes Eis mit Sahne
two or three scoops of ice cream **mit** whipped cream

(dahm) (blahnsh)
Dame Blanche
Vanilleeis mit hot chocolate sauce

After completing your **Essen** (meal), call **den Kellner und** pay just as **Sie haben** already learned in Step 16: **Herr Ober, ich möchte zahlen.**

Unten ist a sample **Speisekarte** to help you prepare for your holiday.

RESTAURANT ZUM GOLDENEN HIRSCHEN

SPEISEKARTE

VORSPEISEN

Nordseekrabben-Cocktail (North Sea shrimp cocktail)	DM 7,00
Matjeshering in saurer Sahne (pickled herring in sour cream)	6,00
Geräucherte Lachsschnitten garniert (smoked salmon)	9,50
Westfälischer Schinken mit Bauernbrot (Westphalian ham with rye bread)	10,00
Gefüllte Eier (deviled eggs)	4,00

SUPPEN

Fleischbrühe mit Ei (clear broth with egg)	2,75
Hühnerbrühe mit Reis (chicken broth with rice)	3,25
Ochsenschwanzsuppe (oxtail soup)	4,00

HAUPTGERICHTE

Filet Mignon mit pommes frites und Spargel (filet mignon with French fries, asparagus)	16,50
Bachforelle blau mit Petersilienkartoffeln und Gurkensalat (blue brook trout with parsley potatoes, cucumber salad)	14,50
Wiener Schnitzel mit Röstkartoffeln und Erbsen (breaded veal cutlet with roasted potatoes, peas)	11,80
Kasseler Rippchen mit Sauerkraut und Kartoffelpüree (smoked pork chops, sauerkraut, mashed potatoes)	9,00
Ungarisches Gulasch mit Butternudeln und gemischten Salat (Hungarian goulash with buttered noodles, mixed salad)	8,50
Sauerbraten mit Rotkraut und Klößen (sauerbraten with red cabbage, dumplings)	12,00
Rehragout mit Pilzen, Eierspätzle und Preiselbeeren (ragout of venison with mushrooms, homemade egg noodles, cranberries)	11,50
Gänsebraten mit Weinkraut und Kartoffelpüree (roasted goose with wine cabbage, mashed potatoes)	15,25
Hühnerfrikassee mit Reis, Bohnen und gemischtem Salat (chicken stew with rice, green beans, mixed salad)	8,50
Gebratenes 1/2 Huhn mit Kartoffelsalat (roasted chicken with potato salad)	8,25
Jägerschnitzel	12,75

NACHSPEISEN

Gemischtes Eis mit Schlagsahne	3,00
Apfelstrudel (apple strudel)	2,90
Käsekuchen (cheese cake)	2,90
Obsttorte (fruit pastry)	2,75
Gemischte Käseplatte mit Brot und Butter (assorted cheeses with bread and butter)	7,50

GETRÄNKE

Weißweine	10,50—31,00
Rotweine	10,50-31,00
Liköre, Weinbrände (liqueurs and brandies)	3,50
Bier	2,25-4,50
Mineralwasser	2,25
Fruchtsäfte (fruit juices)	2,25
Kaffee	2,50-4,00
Tee	3,00

Unsere Preise sind Endpreise einschließlich Bedienungsgeld und Mehrwertsteuer. (Our prices include service and sales tax.)

- ☐ **der Zentimeter** *(tsen-tih-may-tair)*.... centimeter __________
- ☐ **das Zentrum** *(tsen-troom)*............ center __________
- ☐ **die Zeremonie** *(tsair-ih-moh-nee)*...... ceremony __________
- ☐ **die Zigarette** *(tsih-gah-ret-tah)*........ cigarette __________
- ☐ **die Zigarre** *(tsih-gah-rah)*............ cigar __________

Frühstück ist ein bißchen different because **es ist** fairly standardized **und Sie** will frequently take it at your **Pension** *(pawn-tsi-ohn)* as **es ist** included **in dem Preis** of the **Zimmer. Unten ist** a sample of what **Sie können** expect to greet you **am Morgen** (in the morning).

Frühstück 1 .... **DM 3,45**

1 Tasse Kaffee, Tee oder Schokolade
Brot und Brötchen, Butter,
Marmelade und 1 gekochtes Ei

Frühstück 2 .... **DM 4,20**

1 Portion Kaffee, Tee oder Kakao
1 Glas Orangensaft
2 Brötchen, versch. belegt (assorted toppings)

Frühstück 3 .... **DM 4,50**

1 Kännchen Kaffee, Tee oder Schokolade
Butter, Brot und Brötchen
dazu 1 kleine Aufschnittplatte (plate of cold cuts)

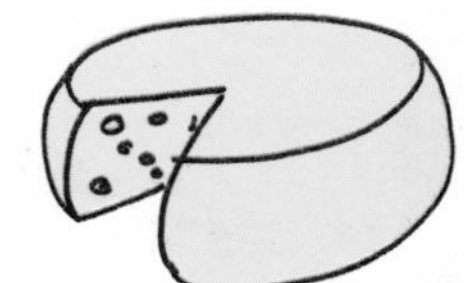

Beilagen zum Frühstück

1 frisch gekochtes Ei .... **DM 0,75**
Frühstücksportion Holländer Käse .... **DM 2,00**
Frühstücksportion gekochter Schinken ..... **DM 2,60**
Frühstücksportion gemischter Aufschnitt ... **DM 3,50**

- ☐ **der Zirkus** *(tsir-koos)* .... circus ____________
- ☐ **die Zivilisation** *(tsih-vih-lih-zah-tsi-ohn)* ..... civilization ____________
- ☐ **der Zoo** *(tsoh)* .... zoo ____________
- ☐ **zu** *(tsoo)* .... to ____________
- ☐ **der Zucker** *(tsoo-kair)* .... sugar ____________

Step 19

(vahs) **Was ist** different about **das Telefon in Deutschland?** Well, **Sie** never notice such things until **Sie** want to use them. **Telefone** allow you to reserve **Hotelzimmer** in another *(shtaht)* **Stadt** (city), call friends, reserve *(tay-ah-tair-kar-ten)* **Theaterkarten, Konzertkarten, oder Ballettkarten**, make emergency calls, check on the hours of a *(moo-zay-oom)* **Museum**, rent **ein Auto, und** all those other **Dinge** which **wir machen** on a daily basis. **Es** also gives you a certain amount of freedom — **Sie können** your own calls **machen**.

Having **ein Telefon in** *(ear-em)* **Ihrem Haus ist nicht** as common **in Deutschland** as **in Amerika**. That means **Sie können** *(tay-lay-fohn-tsel-en)* **Telefonzellen** everywhere **finden**. Since they **sind** state-owned, **sie** (they) sport **die Farbe gelb** just like **die Postkasten.**

Das ist eine deutsche Telefonzelle.

So far, so good. **Nun** let's read the instructions for using **das Telefon.** This **ist** one of those moments when you realize,

Ich bin nicht in Amerika.

So let's learn how to operate **das Telefon.**

This **ist** your first encounter with what **ist** known as **Amtsdeutsch** *(ahmts-doych)* (bureaucratic German). All **es ist, ist** complicated **Wörter für einfache** *(ine-fahk-ah)* (simple) **Wörter.** Some of these **Wörter** you should be able to recognize already. Let's learn the others. Stick to the **Deutsch und Sie** will be fine!

ÖFFENTLICHER MÜNZFERNSPRECHER

Orts- und Ferngespräche

Keine (no) **Telegramme, keine** (no) **Auslandsgespräche**

Handapparat (receiver) **abnehmen** (lift)

Wahlton (dial tone) **abwarten** (wait for)

Mindestens (at least) **20 Pfennig einwerfen** (throw in)

Wählen (dial)

Bei (with) **Ferngesprächen** (long-distance calls) **Vorwahlnummer** (area code) **nicht** (not) **vergessen** (forget)

Nach (after) **beendetem** (completed) **Gespräch** (call)

Handapparat (receiver) **einhängen** (hang up)

Überfall (accident), **Verkehrsunfall** (traffic accident) ________ **110**

Feuer (fire) ________ **112**

Rettungsdienst (rescue service) ________ **112**

Auskunft (information) ________ **118**

Englisch		Deutsch		Amtsdeutsch
the telephone	=	**das Telefon**	=	**der Fernsprecher** **der öffentliche Fernsprecher**
the coin telephone	=	**das Telefon**	=	**der Münzfernsprecher** **der öffentliche Münzfernsprecher**
the telephone booth	=	**die Telefonzelle**	=	**die Fernsprechzelle** **die öffentliche Fernsprechzelle**
the telephone book	=	**das Telefonbuch**	=	**das Fernsprechverzeichnis**
the telephone conversation	=	**das Telefongespräch**	=	**das Ferngespräch** **das Ortsgespräch**
to telephone / call	=	**telefonieren**	=	**anrufen**

So **nun Sie haben** the simple **und** the complicated versions of **das Telefon. Es gibt** area codes **in Deutschland** just as **in Amerika und sie heißen „die Vorwahlnummer."** (for-vahl-noo-mair) A large **Stadt** (shtaht) city like **Frankfurt oder München hat eine Vorwahlnummer** like 060 **oder** 080. Then a portion of the large **Stadt** might have **eine Vorwahlnummer** like 061 **oder** 082. A smaller suburb might be 0613 **oder** 0824, **und** finally, a small town farther away would have **eine Vorwahlnummer** like 06139 **oder** 08241. So just through **die Vorwahlnummer lernen Sie ein bißchen** about the size of the town **Sie telefonieren und** its proximity to a major **Stadt.**

When answering **das Telefon, Sie** pick up **den Handapparat** (hahnt-ah-pah-raht) receiver **und** just say your **Name,** (nah-mah) „Elke Schmidt." When saying good-bye, **Sie sagen, „Auf Wiederhören"** (owf) (vee-dair-hur-en) hear from you again — *not* **„Auf Wiedersehen."** (vee-dair-zay-en) see you again **Hier sind** some sample possibilities **für ein Telefongespräch**. (tay-lay-fohn-ge-shprake) Write them in the blanks **unten.**

Ich möchte Auto Firma Schmidt anrufen. (ow-toh) (fear-mah) (on-roo-fen) ______________________________

Ich möchte Chikago anrufen. Ich möchte Chikago anrufen.

Ich möchte Frau Liebsch in Heidelberg anrufen. (leebsh) ______________________________

Ich möchte Lufthansa in Frankfurt anrufen. (looft-hahn-za) ______________________________

Ich möchte ein R-gespräch machen. (air-ge-shprake) collect call ______________________________

Wo ist eine Telefonzelle? ______________________________

Wo ist das Telefonbuch? ______________________________

Meine Nummer ist 67598. (my-nah) my ______________________________

Was ist die Telefonnummer? ______________________________

 Hier ist another possible **Konversation.** Listen to the **Wörter und wie sie** are used.

Thomas:	**Hallo, hier ist Herr Faber. Ich möchte mit Frau Schirer** *(shy-rair)* **sprechen.**
Sekretärin: *(zeh-kre-tear-in)*	**Einen** (one) **Augenblick** *(ow-gen-bleek)* (moment)**. Ich verbinde** *(fair-bin-dah)* (connect)**. Es tut** *(toot)* **mir leid** *(light)* (I'm sorry)**. Es ist besetzt.**
Thomas:	**Wiederholen** *(vee-dair-hoh-len)* **Sie das bitte. Ich spreche nur ein bißchen Deutsch.**
	Sprechen Sie bitte langsamer *(long-zah-mair)* (slower)**.**
Sekretärin:	**Es tut mir leid. Es ist besetzt.**
Thomas:	**Ah. Danke. Auf Wiederhören** *(vee-dair-hur-en)***.**

Und noch *(nohk)* (still) **eine** possibility . . .

Christina:	**Ich möchte Auskunft** *(ows-koonft)* (information) **für Kassel, bitte. Ich möchte die Telefonnummer für Herrn** *(hairn)* (Mr.) **Doktor** (Dr.) **Friedrich Bopp, bitte.**
Auskunft:	**Die Nummer ist 0881-5552.**
Christina:	**Wiederholen** *(vee-dair-hoh-len)* **Sie das, bitte.**
Auskunft:	**Die Nummer ist 0881-5552.**
Christina:	**Danke. Auf Wiederhören.**

Sie sind nun ready to use any **Telefon in Deutschland**. Just take it **langsam und** speak clearly.

Don't forget that **Sie können fragen . . .**

Was kostet ein Ortsgespräch *(orts-ge-shprake)***?**

Was kostet ein Ortsgespräch?

Was kostet ein Telefongespräch nach Amerika?

____

Was kostet ein Ferngespräch *(fairn-ge-shprake)* **nach Bremen?**

____

Was kostet ein Ferngespräch nach Italien?

____

Don't forget that **Sie brauchen Kleingeld** *(kline-gelt)* **für das Telefon!**

Step 20

(oo-bahn)
die U-Bahn
subway

(oo-bahn) **„U-Bahn“ ist der deutsche Name für** the subway. **Die großen** (large) *(shtay-tah)* **Städte** (cities) **in Deutschland haben eine U-Bahn** just like **die großen** *(shtay-tah)* **Städte in Amerika. Sie** will find **eine U-Bahn in den großen Städten** like *(bohn)* **Bonn,** *(hahm-boorg)* **Hamburg,** *(bear-leen)* **Berlin (Ost und West),** *(frahnk-furt)* **Frankfurt und** *(meuw-shen)* **München. Die kleineren Städte** like *(high-del-bairg)* **Heidelberg,** *(mahn-hime)* **Mannheim, und** *(fry-boorg)* **Freiburg haben eine** *(shtrah-sen-bahn)* **Straßenbahn,** or what we call a streetcar. Both **die U-Bahn und die** *(shtrah-sen-bahn)* **Straßenbahn (S-Bahn) sind** *(ine-fahk)* **einfach** (simple) **und** quick ways to travel. *(vel-chah)* **Welche** (which) **Wörter** *(mew-sen)* **müssen** (must) **Sie für die U-Bahn und die Straßenbahn** *(viss-en)* **wissen** (know)? Let's learn them by practicing them aloud **und dann** by writing them in the blanks **unten.**

(dee) (oo-bahn) **die U-Bahn**

____

(shtrah-sen-bahn) **die Straßenbahn**

____

(boos) **der Bus**

der Bus

(hahl-tah-shtel-ah) **die Haltestelle** = the stop _______________

(lee-nee-ah) **die Linie** = the line die Linie

(shahf-nair) **der Schaffner** = the conductor _______________

Let's also review the "transportation" **Verben** at this point.

(ine-shtai-gen) **einsteigen** = to get in/board

____

(ows-shtai-gen) **aussteigen** = to get out/disembark

aussteigen

(oom-shtai-gen) **umsteigen** = to transfer

____

(ine-shtem-peln) **einstempeln** = to have a ticket stamped

____

Maps displaying the various **Linien** *(lee-nee-en)* **und Haltestellen** *(hahl-tah-shtel-en)* [stops] **sind** generally posted outside every **Eingang** *(ine-gong)* **für die U-Bahn**. Normally **der U-Bahnfahrplan** *(oo-bahn-fahr-plahn)* [subway schedule] **ist** available at a **Fremdenverkehrsamt,** *(frem-den-fair-kairs-ahmt)* [tourist information office] possibly a **Reisebüro, oder** even a **Kiosk** *(key-ohsk)* [newsstand]. Just as **in Amerika, die Linien sind** frequently color-coded to make the **Fahrplan** [schedule] **sehr einfach** to **verstehen** *(fair-shtay-en)*. Other than having foreign **Wörter, deutsche U-Bahnen sind** just like **amerikanische U-Bahnen.** Check the **Name** of the last **Haltestelle** on the **Linie** which you should take **und** catch the **U-Bahn** traveling in that direction. The same applies for the **Straßenbahn**. See the **Fahrplan unten.**

The same basic set of **Wörter und Fragen** will see you through traveling **mit dem Bus, mit der U-Bahn, mit der Straßenbahn, oder** even **mit dem Zug.**

Naturally, **die** *(air-stah)* **erste** (first) **Frage ist ,,wo":**

Wo **ist die** *(oo-bahn-hahl-tah-shtel-ah)* **U-Bahnhaltestelle?**

Wo **ist die** *(shtrah-sen-bahn-hahl-tah-shtel-ah)* **Straßenbahnhaltestelle?**

Wo **ist die** *(boos-hahl-tah-shtel-ah)* **Bushaltestelle?**

Practice the following basic **Fragen** out loud **und dann** write them in the blanks *(rex)* **rechts.**

1. **Wo ist die U-Bahnhaltestelle?** ____________________

   Wo ist die Straßenbahnhaltestelle? ____________________

   Wo ist die Bushaltestelle? Wo ist die Bushaltestelle?

2. *(vee)* **Wie oft geht die U-Bahn?** ____________________

   Wie oft geht die Straßenbahn? ____________________

   Wie oft geht der Bus? ____________________

3. *(vahn)* **Wann geht die U-Bahn?** ____________________

   Wann geht die Straßenbahn? ____________________

   Wann geht der Bus? ____________________

4. *(gate)* **Geht die U-Bahn nach** *(noy-en-hime)* **Neuenheim?** ____________________

   Geht die Straßenbahn nach Neunheim? ____________________

   Geht der Bus nach Neuenheim? Geht der Bus nach Neuenheim?

5. *(vahs)* **Was kostet eine Fahrkarte** (ticket) **für die U-Bahn?** ____________________

   Was kostet eine Fahrkarte für die Straßenbahn? ____________________

   Was kostet eine Fahrkarte für den Bus? ____________________

Nun that **Sie haben** got into the swing of things, practice the following patterns aloud, substituting ,,**Straßenbahn**" for ,,**U-Bahn,**" **und** so on.

1. **Wo kaufe ich eine Fahrkarte für die U-Bahn? für die Straßenbahn? für den Bus?**

2. **Wann geht die U-Bahn nach Sachsenhausen?** *(zahk-zen-how-zen)* **nach Altenheim?** *(ahl-ten-hime)* **nach Oppenheim?** *(oh-pen-hime)*
   zur Stadtmitte? *(shtaht-mit-tah)* city middle **zum Zentrum?** *(tsen-troom)* center **zur Universität?** *(oo-ni-vair-zi-tate)* university **nach Dahlem? nach Godesberg?** *(goh-des-bairg)*

3. **Wo ist die Haltestelle für die U-Bahn nach Sachsenhausen?**

   Wo ist die Haltestelle für die Straßenbahn nach Altenheim?

   Wo ist die Haltestelle für den Bus nach Oppenheim?

   Wo ist die Haltestelle für die U-Bahn zur *(tsoor)* to the **Stadtmitte?**

   Wo ist die Haltestelle für die Straßenbahn zum *(tsoom)* to the **Zentrum?**

   Wo ist die Haltestelle für den Bus nach Dahlem?

   Wo ist die Haltestelle für die U-Bahn nach Godesberg?

Lesen Sie *(lay-zen)* read the following **typische** *(two-pish-ah)* **Konversation und dann schreiben** *(shry-ben)* **Sie die Konversation** in the blanks **rechts.**

Welche *(vel-chah)* which **Linie** *(lee-nee-ah)* **geht nach Charlottenburg?** ____________________

Die rote Linie geht nach Charlottenburg. ____________________

Wie oft geht die rote Linie? ____________________

Alle *(ahl-ah)* every **zehn Minuten.** Alle zehn Minuten.

Muß ich umsteigen? ____________________

Ja, in der Stadtmitte. Sie steigen an at **der Haltestelle „Stadtmitte" um.**

____

Wie lange dauert es von *(fohn)* from **hier nach Charlottenburg?** ____________________

Es dauert 20 Minuten. ____________________

Was kostet eine Fahrkarte nach Charlottenburg? ____________________

Eine Mark neunzig. Eine Mark neunzig.

Können Sie the following thoughts into **Deutsch** translate? **Die** *(ahnt-vor-ten)* **Antworten** (answers) **sind unten.**

1. Where is the subway stop? ____________________
2. What costs a ticket to Neuenheim? ____________________
3. How often goes the yellow line to Weinheim? ____________________
4. Where buy I a ticket to the city center? ____________________
5. Where is the streetcar stop? ____________________
6. I would like to get out. Ich möchte aussteigen.
7. Must I transfer? ____________________
8. Where must I transfer? ____________________

Hier sind drei Verben mehr.

(vah-shen) **waschen** = to wash

(fair-lear-en) **verlieren** = to lose

(dow-airn) **dauern** = to last

waschen ____________________ ____________________

Sie know the basic "plug-in" formula, so translate the following thoughts **mit** these **neuen Verben. Die** *(ahnt-vor-ten)* **Antworten sind auch unten.**

1. I wash the jacket. Ich wasche die Jacke.
2. You lose the book. ____________________
3. It takes (lasts) 20 minutes to Charlottenburg. ____________________
4. It takes three hours with a car. ____________________

ANTWORTEN

1. **Wo ist die U-Bahnhaltestelle?**
2. **Was kostet (wieviel kostet) eine Karte nach Neuenheim?**
3. **Wie oft geht die gelbe Linie nach Weinheim?**
4. **Wo kaufe ich eine Karte zur Stadtmitte (zum Zentrum)?**
5. **Wo ist die Straßenbahnhaltestelle?**
6. **Ich möchte aussteigen.**
7. **Muß ich umsteigen?**
8. **Wo muß ich umsteigen?**

1. **Ich wasche die Jacke.**
2. **Sie verlieren das Buch.**
3. **Es dauert zwanzig Minuten nach Charlottenburg.**
4. **Es dauert drei Stunden mit dem Auto.**

(fair-kow-fen) Verkaufen *(selling)* und *(kow-fen)* Kaufen *(buying)*

Step 21

Shopping abroad **ist** exciting. The simple everyday task of buying **einen** *(lee-tair)* **Liter Milch oder einen** *(ahp-fel)* **Apfel** *(apple)* becomes a challenge that **Sie** should **nun** be able to meet quickly **und** easily. Of course, **Sie** will purchase *(on-denk-en)* **Andenken** *(souvenirs)*, **Briefmarken, und Postkarten,** but do not forget those many other **Dinge** ranging from shoelaces to aspirin that **Sie** might need unexpectedly. *(viss-en)* **Wissen** *(know)* **Sie** the difference between **einer** *(boohk-hahnt-loong)* **Buchhandlung** *(bookstore)* **und einer** *(ah-poh-tay-kah)* **Apotheke?** *(pharmacy)* **Nein.** Let's learn about the different *(ge-shef-tah)* **Geschäfte** *(shops)* **und** *(lay-den)* **Läden** *(stores)* **in Deutschland. Unten ist ein** *(shtaht-plahn)* **Stadtplan** *(map)* **für eine** *(two-pish-ah)* **typische deutsche Stadt** *(city)*.

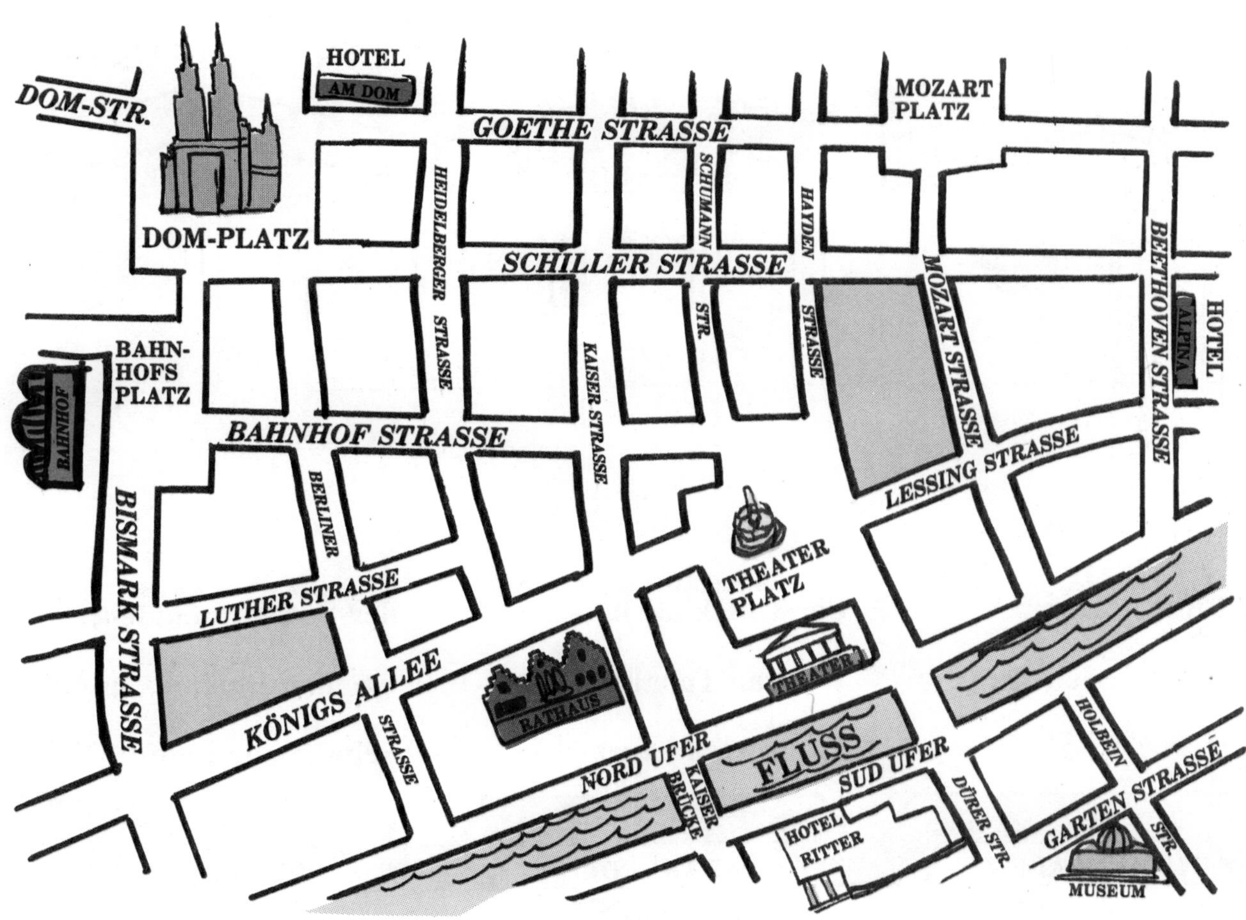

Auf den *(nex-sten)* **nächsten Seiten** *(pages)* **sind die Geschäfte** *(shops)* **in** *(dee-zair)* **dieser** *(this)* **Stadt.** Be sure to fill in the blanks **unter den Bildern mit den Namen** of the *(ge-shef-tah)* **Geschäfte.**

(beck-air-eye)
die Bäckerei,

(mahn) (kowft)
wo man Brot kauft
one buys

(mets-gair-eye)
die Metzgerei,

(flysh)
wo man Fleisch kauft
one meat

(vesh-air-eye)
die Wäscherei,

(kly-dair) (vesht)
wo man Kleider wäscht
clothes washes

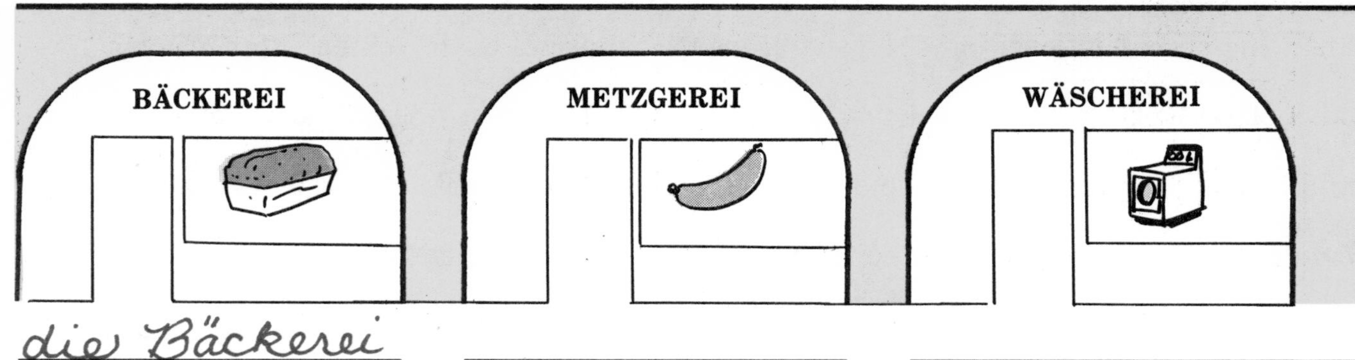

die Bäckerei

(kohn-dee-tor-eye)
die Konditorei,
café

wo man Kaffee trinkt

(droh-gih-ree)
die Drogerie,
drugstore

(zigh-fah)
wo man Seife kauft

(ah-poh-tay-kah)
die Apotheke,
pharmacy

(ahs-peer-een)
wo man Aspirin kauft
aspirin

die Apotheke

(bloo-men-lah-den)
der Blumenladen,
flower shop

wo man Blumen kauft

(tah-bahk-lah-den)
der Tabakladen,

wo man Tabak und

(tsih-gah-ret-ten)
Zigaretten kauft

(zews-vah-ren-lah-den)
der Süßwarenladen,
candy store

(bohn-bohns)
wo man Bonbons und

Schokolade kauft

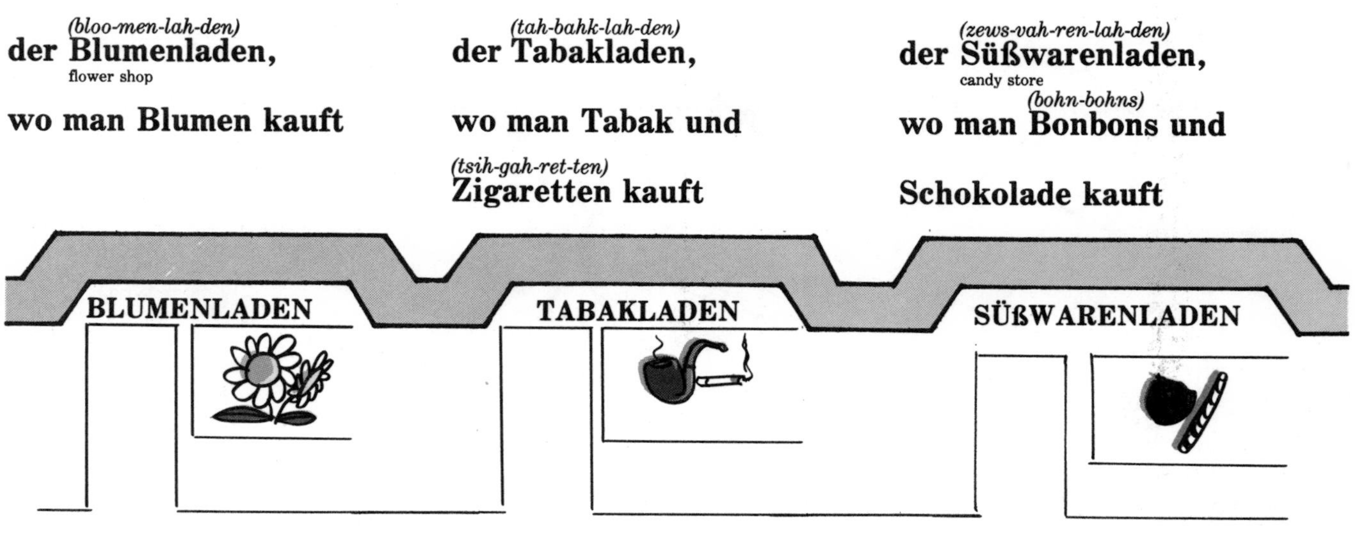

(milsh-ge-sheft)
das Milchgeschäft, dairy
(mahn)
wo man Milch kauft

(foh-toh-ge-sheft)
das Fotogeschäft, camera store
wo man Film kauft

(ge-mew-zah-ge-sheft)
das Gemüsegeschäft, vegetable store
wo man Gemüse kauft

(park-plahts)
der Parkplatz, parking lot
(mahn)
wo man Autos parkt

(frih-zur)
der Friseur, hairdresser
(shny-det)
wo man Haar schneidet (cuts)

(shny-dair)
der Schneider, tailor
(kly-dair)
wo man Kleider macht (clothes, makes)

(post-ahmt)
das Postamt, post office
wo man Briefmarken kauft

(poh-lih-tsigh-ahmt)
das Polizeiamt, police station
wo man die Polizei findet

(bahnk)
die Bank,
(vex-selt)
wo man Geld wechselt und (exchanges)
(sheck) (ine-lurst)
man einen Scheck einlöst (check, cashes)

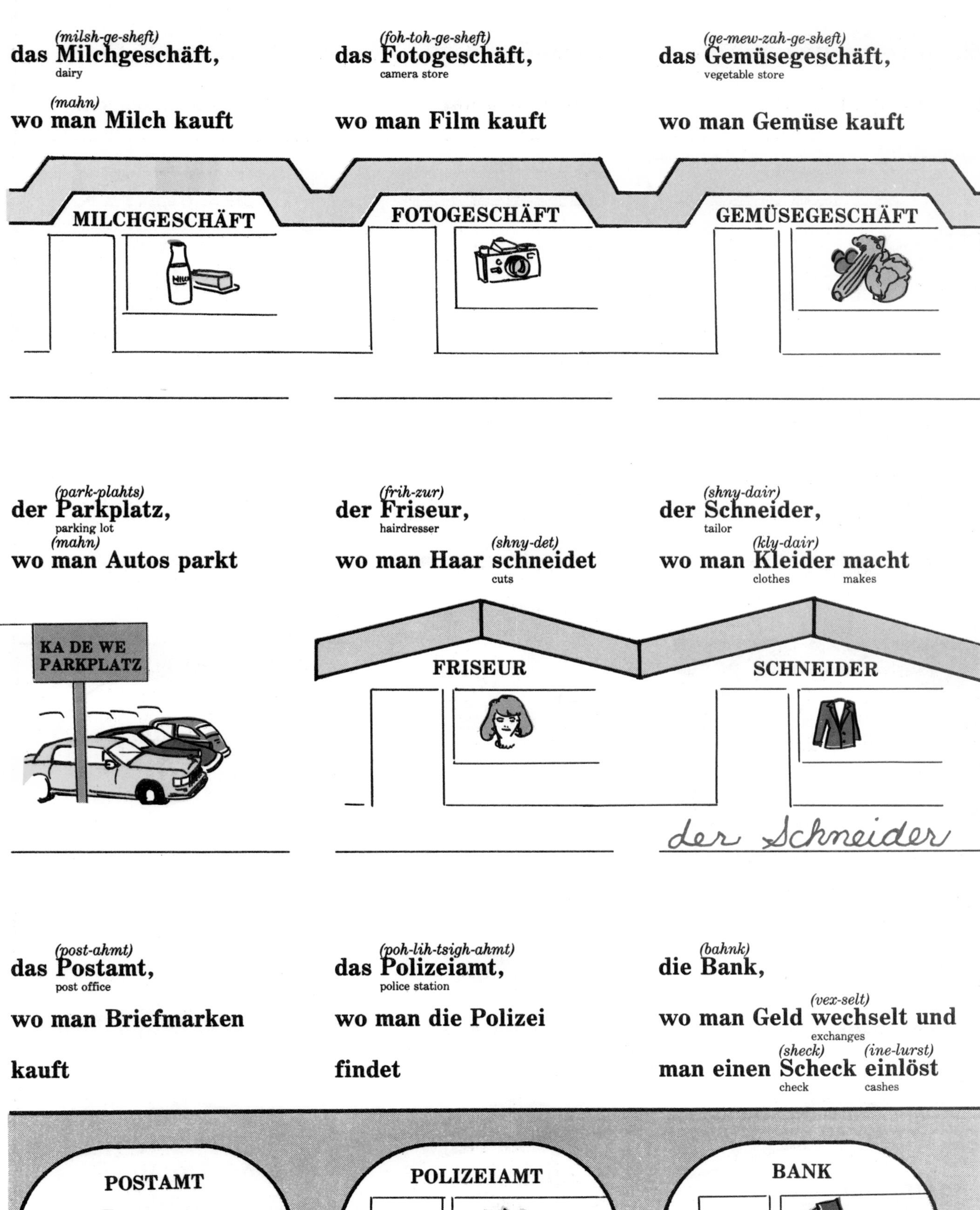

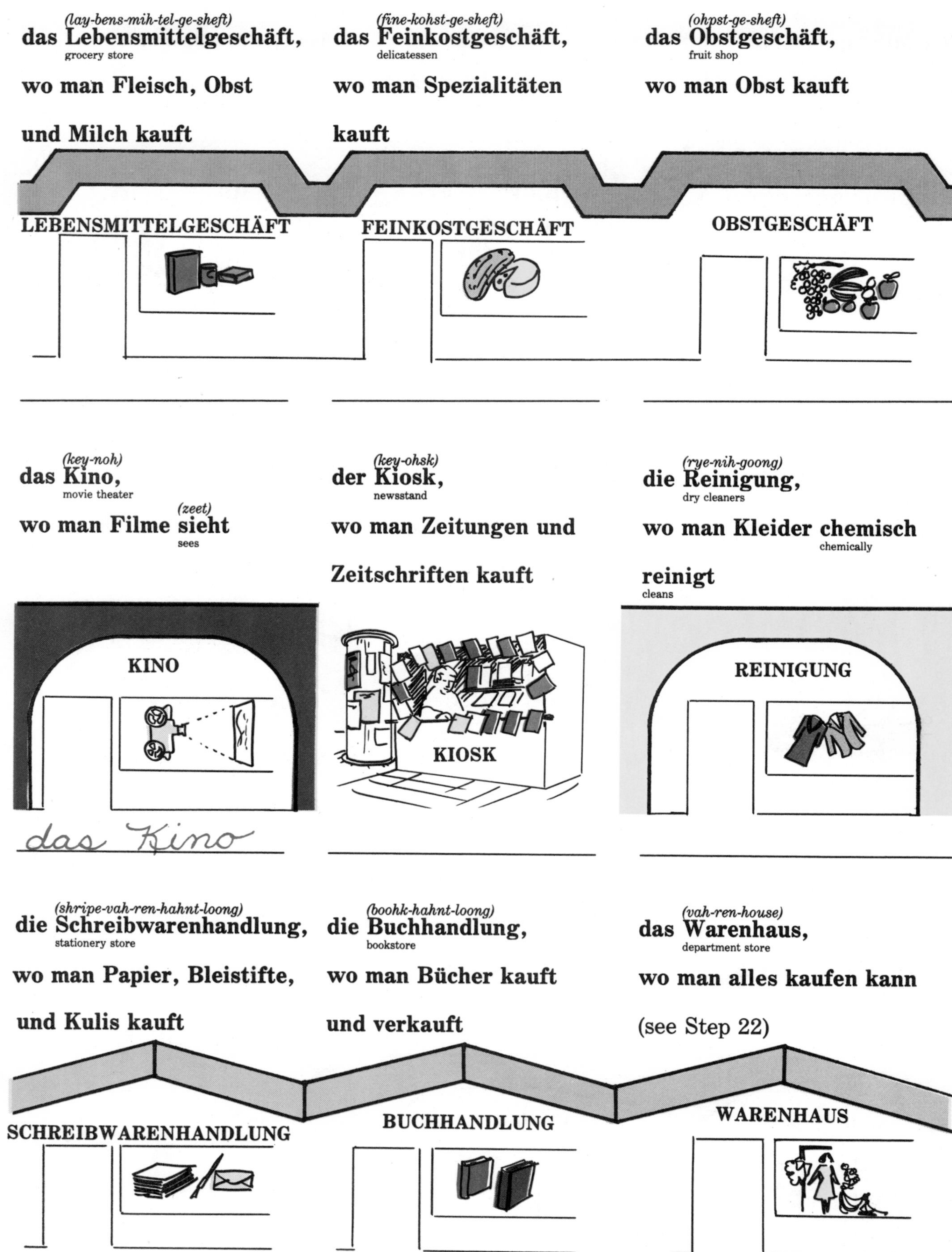
(lay-bens-mih-tel-ge-sheft)
das Lebensmittelgeschäft,
grocery store
wo man Fleisch, Obst
und Milch kauft
(fine-kohst-ge-sheft)
das Feinkostgeschäft,
delicatessen
wo man Spezialitäten
kauft
(ohpst-ge-sheft)
das Obstgeschäft,
fruit shop
wo man Obst kauft
LEBENSMITTELGESCHÄFT
FEINKOSTGESCHÄFT
OBSTGESCHÄFT
(key-noh)
das Kino,
movie theater
wo man Filme sieht (zeet)
sees
(key-ohsk)
der Kiosk,
newsstand
wo man Zeitungen und
Zeitschriften kauft
(rye-nih-goong)
die Reinigung,
dry cleaners
wo man Kleider chemisch
chemically
reinigt
cleans
KINO
KIOSK
REINIGUNG
das Kino
(shripe-vah-ren-hahnt-loong)
die Schreibwarenhandlung,
stationery store
wo man Papier, Bleistifte,
und Kulis kauft
(boohk-hahnt-loong)
die Buchhandlung,
bookstore
wo man Bücher kauft
und verkauft
(vah-ren-house)
das Warenhaus,
department store
wo man alles kaufen kann
(see Step 22)
SCHREIBWARENHANDLUNG
BUCHHANDLUNG
WARENHAUS

(markt)
der Markt, wo man
market

Gemüse und Obst kauft

(on-denk-en-lah-den)
der Andenkenladen,
souvenir store

wo man Andenken kauft

(tahnk-shtel-ah)
die Tankstelle,
gas station

wo man Benzin kauft

die Tankstelle

(ry-zah-bew-roh)
das Reisebüro,
travel office

wo man Flugkarten kauft

(uhr-mah-kair)
der Uhrmacher,
watchmaker

wo man Uhren kauft

(fish-hahnt-loong)
die Fischhandlung,
fish store

wo man Fisch kauft

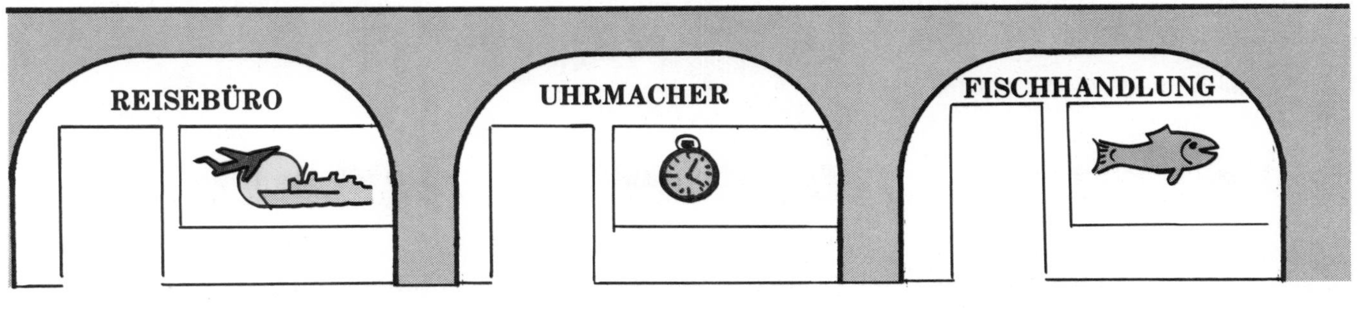

(vahn) **Wann** sind die deutschen Geschäfte **auf** (open)? Normally, **die deutschen Geschäfte sind Montag bis** (until) **Freitag, von** (fohn) **8:00 oder 9:00 Uhr bis 18 Uhr 30 auf. Viele** (many) **Geschäfte** will close over the lunch hour **(12:00 bis 14:00),** so plan accordingly. **Am Samstag sind die Geschäfte von 8:00 oder 9:00 Uhr nur bis 14:00 Uhr auf. Am Sonntag sind die Geschäfte zu** (tsoo) (closed)**!** On the first **Samstag** of every **Monat,** there is what is known as **„langer** (long-air) (long) **Samstag.“** On this **Samstag, die Geschäfte bleiben** (bly-ben) (remain) **bis 18:00 Uhr auf. Gibt es** (is there) anything else which makes **deutsche Geschäfte** different from **amerikanische Geschäfte? Ja.** Look at **das Bild auf der nächsten Seite.**

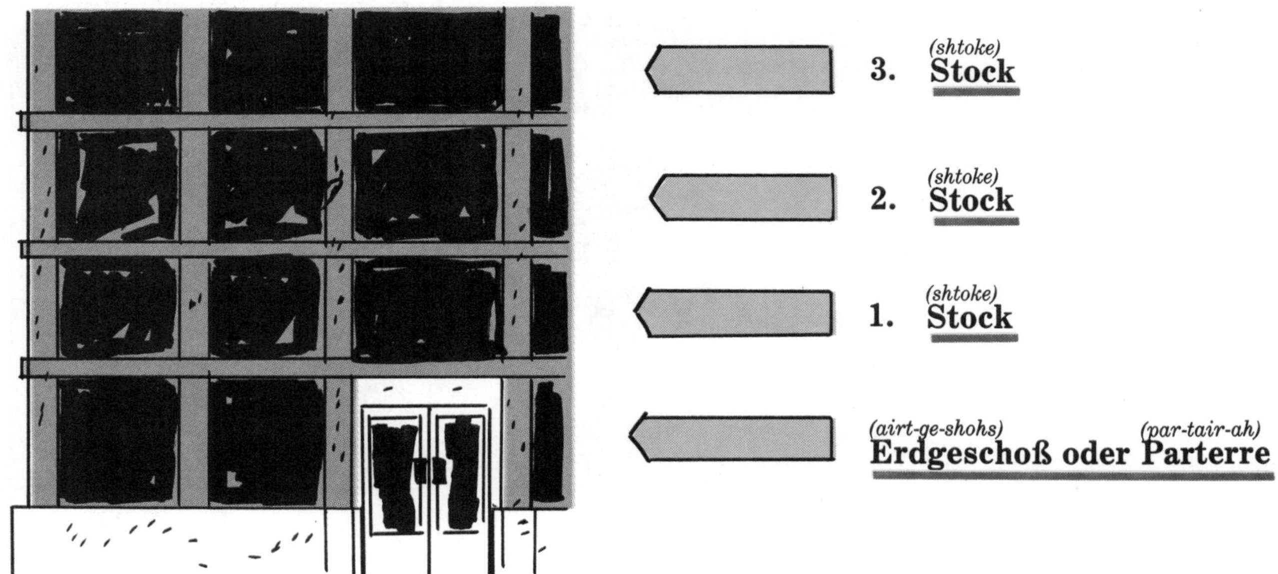

In Deutschland, the ground floor **heißt** exactly that — **das** (airt-ge-shohs) **Erdgeschoß** (earth floor). The first floor **ist** the next floor up **und** so on. Now that **Sie** know **die Namen für die deutschen Geschäfte,** let's practice shopping.

I. First step — **Wo!**

Wo ist das Milchgeschäft? **Wo ist die Bank?** **Wo ist das Kino?**

Go through **die Geschäfte** introduced in this Step **und** ask **„wo"** **mit** each **Geschäft.** Another way of asking **wo** is to ask

Gibt es (is there) **ein Milchgeschäft in der** (the) (nay-ah) **Nähe** (vicinity)**?** **Gibt es eine Bank in der Nähe?**

Go through **die Geschäfte** again using this new question.

II. Next step — tell them **was Sie** are looking for, **brauchen oder möchten!**

1) **Ich brauche . . .** Ich brauche ______________________

2) **Haben Sie . . . ?** ______________________

3) **Ich möchte . . .** ______________________

Ich brauche einen Bleistift.

Haben Sie einen Bleistift?

Ich möchte einen Bleistift.

Ich brauche einen Liter Buttermilch.

Haben Sie einen Liter Buttermilch?

Ich möchte einen Liter Buttermilch.

Go through the glossary at the end of this **Buch und** select **zwanzig** *(tsvahn-tsig)* (twenty) **Wörter.** Drill the above patterns **mit diesen zwanzig Wörtern.** Don't cheat. Drill them **heute. Nun,** take **zwanzig Wörter mehr von Ihrem** *(ear-em)* (your) **Wörterbuch** *(vur-tair-boohk)* (dictionary) **und** do the same.

III. Next step — find out **wieviel es kostet.**

1) **Was** *(vahs)* **kostet das?** ____________________

2) **Wieviel** *(vee-feel)* **kostet das?** ____________________

Was kostet der Bleistift?

Wieviel kostet der Bleistift?

Was kostet der Liter Buttermilch?

Wieviel kostet der Liter Buttermilch?

Using the same **Wörter** that **Sie** selected **oben,** drill **diese Fragen auch.**

IV. If **Sie wissen nicht, wo** to find something, **Sie fragen**

Wo kann ich Aspirin *(ahs-peer-een)* (aspirin) **kaufen?**

Wo kann ich eine Sonnenbrille *(zoh-nen-bril-ah)* (sunglasses) **kaufen?**

Once **Sie finden was Sie** would like, **Sie sagen, Ich möchte das, bitte.**

Oder, if **Sie** would not like **es, Ich möchte das nicht.**

Sie sind nun all set to shop for anything!

Step 22

At this point, **Sie** should just about be ready for your *(ry-zah)* **Reise nach Deutschland. Sie** have gone shopping for those last-minute odds 'n ends. Most likely, the store directory at your local *(vah-ren-house)* **Warenhaus** did **nicht** look like the one **unten! Viele Wörter wissen** (know) **Sie** already **und Sie** could guess at **viele** others. **Sie wissen** that **„Kinder" ist das deutsche Wort für** "children," so if **Sie brauchen** something **für das Kind, Sie** would probably look on *(shtoke)* **Stock zwei oder** *(dry)* **drei, nicht wahr?**

6. STOCK	Brot-Backwaren Cafeteria Delikatessen Spirituosen	Geflügel Lebensmittel Obst Gemüse	Tiefkühlkost Weine Wild Fleisch
5. STOCK	Betten Bettfedern Plastik	Kleinmöbel Lampen Orient	Teppiche Bilder
4. STOCK	Bestecke Elektro-Artikel Glas	Haushaltwaren Hobby Küchenmöbel	Schlüsselbar Keramik Porzellan
3. STOCK	Bücher Fernsehen Kindermöbel Kinderwagen	Spielwaren Musikinstrumente Rundfunk Schreibwaren Schallplatten	Tabakwaren Teeraum Zeitschriften Zeitungen
2. STOCK	Alles für das Kind Damenbekleidung	Herrenbekleidung Damenhüte	Fundbüro Kundendienst
1. STOCK	Autozubehör Damenwäsche Taschentücher	Badeartikel Schuhe Handarbeiten	Bettwäsche Sportartikel
E	Foto-Optik Herrenhüte Schirme Schmuck	Handschuhe Lederwaren Strümpfe Uhren	Herrenartikel Parfümerie Süßwaren

Let's start a check list **für Ihre Reise.** Besides *(kly-dair)* **Kleider** (clothing)**, was brauchen Sie?**

Was *(nay-men)* **nehmen** (take) **Sie nach Europa?**

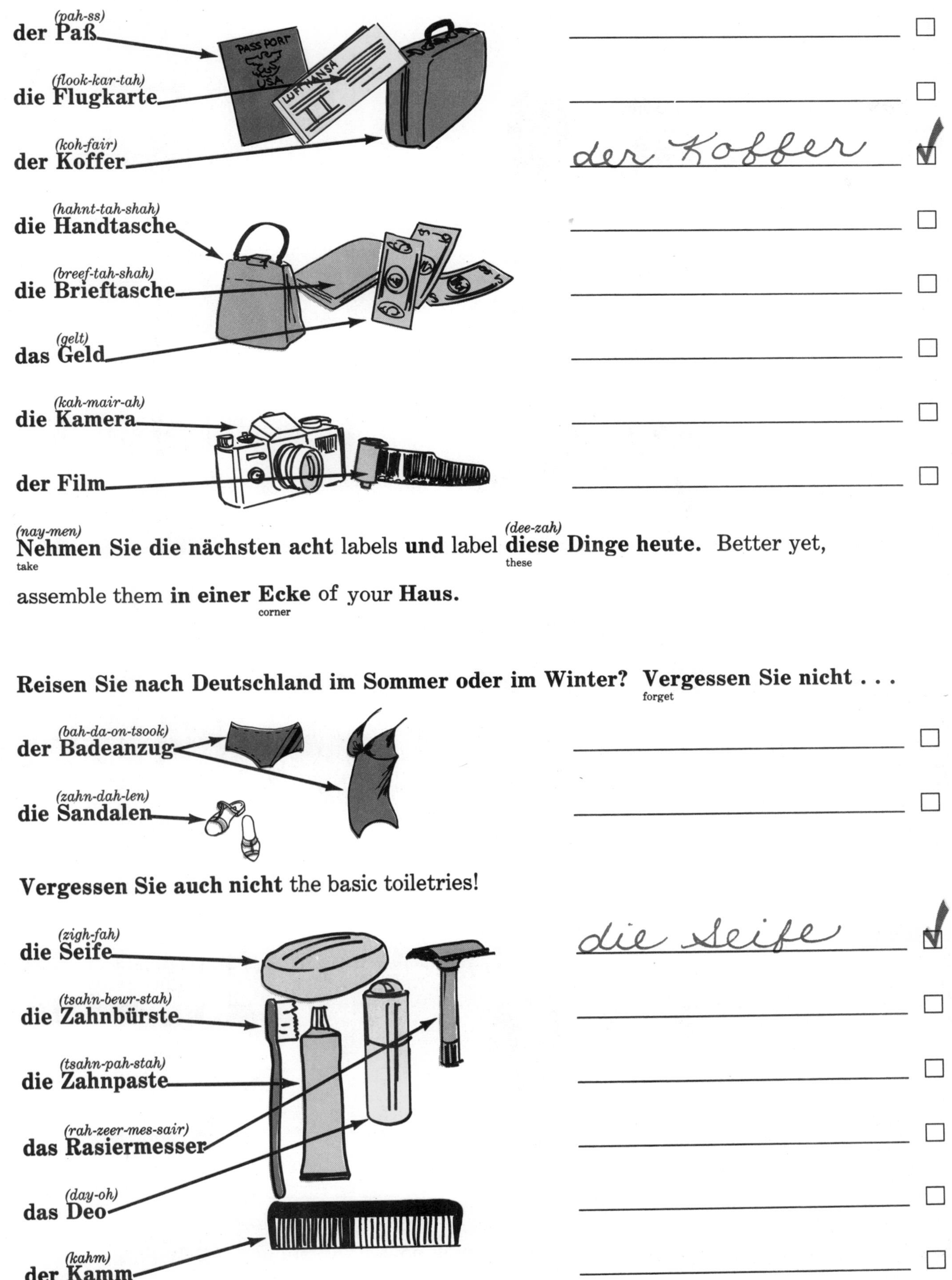

der Paß *(pah-ss)*

die Flugkarte *(flook-kar-tah)*

der Koffer *(koh-fair)* — der Koffer ✓

die Handtasche *(hahnt-tah-shah)*

die Brieftasche *(breef-tah-shah)*

das Geld *(gelt)*

die Kamera *(kah-mair-ah)*

der Film

Nehmen *(nay-men)* (take) **Sie die nächsten acht** labels **und** label **diese** *(dee-zah)* (these) **Dinge heute.** Better yet, assemble them **in einer Ecke** (corner) of your **Haus.**

Reisen Sie nach Deutschland im Sommer oder im Winter? Vergessen (forget) **Sie nicht . . .**

der Badeanzug *(bah-da-on-tsook)*

die Sandalen *(zahn-dah-len)*

Vergessen Sie auch nicht the basic toiletries!

die Seife *(zigh-fah)* — die Seife ✓

die Zahnbürste *(tsahn-bewr-stah)*

die Zahnpaste *(tsahn-pah-stah)*

das Rasiermesser *(rah-zeer-mes-sair)*

das Deo *(day-oh)*

der Kamm *(kahm)*

For the rest of the **Dinge,** let's start **mit** the outside layers **und** work our way in.

(mahn-tel)
der Mantel — der Mantel ✓

(ray-gen-mahn-tel)
der Regenmantel ☐

(ray-gen-shirm)
der Regenschirm ☐

(hahnt-shoo-ah)
die Handschuhe ☐

(hoot)
der Hut ☐

(shtee-fel)
die Stiefel ☐

(shoo-ah)
die Schuhe ☐

(zoh-ken)
die Socken — die Socken ✓

(shtroompf-hoh-zah)
die Strumpfhose ☐

(nay-men) **Nehmen** (take) **Sie die nächsten fünfzehn** labels **und** label **diese Dinge.** Check **und** make sure that **sie sind** *(zow-bair)* **sauber** (clean) **und** ready for your trip. Be sure to do the same **mit** the rest of the **Dinge Sie** *(pah-ken)* **packen** (pack). Check them off on this **Liste** as **Sie** organize them. From **nun** on, **Sie haben** **„Zahnpaste"** **und nicht** "toothpaste."

(shlahf-on-tsook)
der Schlafanzug ☐

(nahkt-hemt)
das Nachthemd ☐

(bah-da-mahn-tel)
der Bademantel ☐

(house-shoo-ah)
die Hausschuhe ☐

Der Bademantel und die Hausschuhe können auch double **für Sie** at the *(shvim-baht)* **Schwimmbad!** (swimming pool)

Having assembled **diese Dinge, Sie sind** ready **für Ihre Reise.** However, being human means occasionally forgetting something. Look again at the **Warenhaus** directory.

Im welchem (which) *(shtoke)* **Stock finden Sie . . .**

Kleider für einen Mann?	**Im** __________ **Stock.**
einen Hut für eine Dame (Frau)?	**Im** __________ **Stock.**
Bücher?	**Im** 3 **Stock.**
(dah-men-vesh-ah) **Damenwäsche?** (ladies' underclothing)	**Im** __________ **Stock.**

Schuhe? **Im** ____________ **Stock.**

Socken (Strümpfe)? **Im** ____________ **Stock.**

Kleider für die Dame? **Im** ____________ **Stock.**

Nun, just remember your basic **Fragen. Wiederholen Sie die typische Konversation unten** out loud **und dann** by filling in the blanks.

Wo finde ich eine Damenhose? ____________________

In der Damenabteilung. ____________________
women's department

Wo ist die Damenabteilung? ____________________

Im zweiten Stock. Im zweiten Stock.

Wo finde ich Seife und Zahnpaste? ____________________

Im Erdgeschoß. ____________________

(tsoo)
Vergessen Sie auch nicht zu fragen . . .
to

Wo ist der Fahrstuhl? ____________________
elevator

Wo ist die Treppe? ____________________
steps

Wo ist die Rolltreppe? ____________________
escalator

Whether **Sie brauchen eine Damenhose oder ein Herrenhemd, die** necessary **Wörter sind** the same! Practice your **neue Wörter mit** the following *(kly-dair)* **Kleider** (clothing). **Wo ist die Bluse?**

Wo ist...

(vel-chah) (grur-sah)
Welche Größe?
which size

____

Es paßt.
It fits

____

Es paßt nicht.
It fits not

Es paßt nicht.

Ich (nay-mah) **nehme dieses.**
take this

____

Was kostet das?

____

Das ist alles. Danke.
all

____

Clothing Sizes: **FRAUEN**

Schuhe

American	5	5½	6	6½	7	7½	8	8½	9
Continental	35	35	36	37	38	38	38	39	40

Kleider

American	8	10	12	14	16	18
Continental	36	38	40	42	44	46

Blusen, Pullis

American	32	34	36	38	40	42	44
Continental	40	42	44	46	48	50	52

Clothing Sizes: **HERREN**

Schuhe

American	7	7½	8	8½	9	9½	10	10½	11	11½
Continental	39	40	41	42	43	43	44	44	45	45

Kleider

American	34	36	38	40	42	44	46	48
Continental	44	46	48	50	52	54	56	58

Hemden

American	14	14½	15	15½	16	16½	17	17½
Continental	36	37	38	39	40	41	42	43

Nun, Sie sind ready **für Ihre Reise. Sie wissen alles, was Sie brauchen.** The next Step will give you a quick review of international road signs **und** then **Sie** are off to the **Flughafen.**

Gute Reise! Viel Spaß!

Step 23

= **Dangerous Intersection**

Hier sind some of the most important **deutsche** *(shtrah-sen-shill-dair)* **Straßenschildern** (street signs). **Fahren Sie** *(for-zeehk-teeg)* **vorsichtig** (carefully)**!**

Gute Reise!

Danger

Dangerous curve

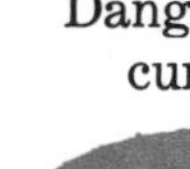

Dangerous intersection

Closed to all vehicles

Prohibited for motor vehicles

Prohibited for motor vehicles on Sundays and holidays

No entry

Stop

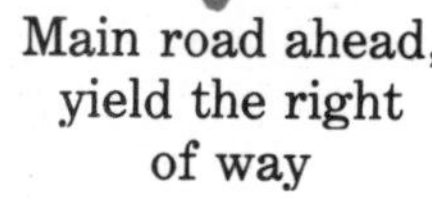

Main road ahead, yield the right of way

You have the right of way

Additional sign indicating the right of way

One-way street

Dead-end street

Detour

Traffic circle

No left turn

No U-turn

No parking

No parking or waiting

No passing

Speed limit

End of speed limit

Beginning of **Autobahn**

Railroad crossing
240 meters

Railroad crossing
160 meters

Railroad crossing
80 meters

Customs

Federal Highway
Number

City limit
(50 km/h speed
limit)

Parking permitted

Road ends, water
ahead

GLOSSARY

A

ab . . . away from, leaves
Abend, der . . . evening
Abendessen, das . . . dinner
abends . . . evenings
abfahren . . . to depart
Abfahrt, die . . . departure
abnehmen . . . to remove
Abteil, das . . . compartment
Abteilung, die . . . department
abwarten . . . to wait for
acht . . . eight
achtzehn . . . eighteen
achtzig . . . eighty
Adresse, die . . . address
alle . . . all, everyone
alles . . . everything
Alphabet, das . . . alphabet
alt . . . old
am (= an dem) . . . at the, on the
Amerika, das . . . America
Amerikaner, der . . . American
amerikanisch . . . American
Amtsdeutsch, das . . bureaucratic German
an . . . on, at, arrives
Andenken, das (die Andenken) . souvenir
Andenkenladen, der . . . souvenir shop
ankommen . . . to arrive
Ankunft, die . . . arrival
Anruf, der . . . call, telephone call
anrufen . . . to call up
Antwort, die (die Antworten) . . . answer
Anzug, der . . . suit
Apfel, der . . . apple
Apotheke, die . . . pharmacy
Appetit, der . . . appetite
April, der . . . April
arbeiten . . . to work
arm . . . poor
Arzt, der . . . physician
auch . . . also
auf . . . on top of, open
auf Deutsch . . . in German
auf Englisch . . . in English
Auf Wiederhören! . . Hear from you again!
Auf Wiedersehen! . . . See you again!
Aufschnittplatte, die . . . cold cut plate
Augenblick, der . . . moment
August, der . . . August
aus . . . out of, from
Ausfahrt, die . . . exit (for vehicles)
Ausgang, der . . . exit (for people)
Auskunft, die . . . information
ausland . . . abroad
Ausland, das . . . foreign country
Auslandsgespräche, die . phone calls to a foreign country
aussteigen . . . to get out
Auto, das (die Autos) . . . car
Autobahn, die . . . freeway
Autoreise, die . . . car trip

B

BH, der . . . brassiere
Bäckerei, die . . . bakery
Backteig, der . . . batter
Badeanzug, der . . . bathing suit
Bademantel, der . . . bathrobe
baden . . . to bathe
Badetuch, das . . . bath towel
Badezimmer, das . . . bathroom
Bahnhof, der . . . train station
Bahnsteig, der . . . railway platform
Ball, der . . . ball
Ballettkarte, die . . . ballet ticket
Banane, die . . . banana
Bank, die . . . bank
Beefsteak, das . . . beefsteak
beendetem . . . concluded
beginnen . . . to begin
bei . . . by, near
Beilagen, die . . . supplements
belegt . . . toppings
Bemerkungen, die . . . remarks, notes
Benzin, das . . . gasoline
Berg, der (die Berge) . . . mountain
besetzt . . . occupied
besser . . . better
bestellen . . . to order
Bett, das . . . bed
Bettdecke, die . . . blanket, bedspread
bezahlen . . . to pay
Bier, das (die Biere) . . . beer
Bierhalle, die . . . beerhall
Bild, das (die Bilder) . . . picture
billig . . . cheap
bin . . . am
bis . . . until
bitte . . . please
blau, blaue . . . blue
bleiben . . . to remain, stay
Bleistift, der . . . pencil
Blume, die (die Blumen) . . . flower
Blumenladen, der . . . flower shop
Bluse, die (die Blusen) . . . blouse
Bonbons, die . . . candy
Boot, das . . . boat
brauchen . . . to need
braun . . . brown
Brief, der (die Briefe) . . . letter
Briefkasten, der . . . mailbox
Briefmarke, die . . . stamp
Brieftasche, die . . . wallet, pocketbook
Brille, die . . . eyeglasses
bringen . . . to bring
Brot, das . . . bread
Brötchen, das . . . roll
Bruder, der . . . brother
Buch, das (die Bücher) . . . book
buchen . . . to book, reserve
Buchhandlung, die . . . bookstore
bunt . . . multi-colored
Büro, das . . . office, study
Bus, der (die Busse) . . . bus
Bushaltestelle, die . . . bus stop
Butter, die . . . butter
Buttermilch, die . . . buttermilk

C

Café, das . . . café
Celsius . . . centigrade

D

DM . . . abbre. for German mark
D-Zug, der . . . express train
Dame, die (die Damen) . . . lady
Damenabteilung, die . . . women's department
Damenhose, die . . . ladies' pants
Damenwäsche, die . . . women's underclothing
danke . . . thank you
Danke schön! . . . Thank you very much!
dann . . . then
das . . . the, that
dauert/dauern . . . lasts/to take time
dazu . . . besides
Decke, die . . . ceiling, cover
dem . . . the
den . . . the
Deo, das . . . deodorant
der . . . the, of the
des . . . the, of the
Deutsch, das . . . German
deutsch, deutschen . . . German
Deutsche Mark, die . . . German mark
Deutschland, das . . . Germany
Dezember, der . . . December
dick . . . thick
die . . . the
Dienstag, der . . . Tuesday
dieser, diesen . . . this, that, these
Ding, das (die Dinge) . . . thing
Doktor, der . . . doctor
Dollar, der . . . dollar
Donnerstag, der . . . Thursday
dort . . . there
drei . . . three
dreißig . . . thirty
dreizehn . . . thirteen
Drogerie, die . . . drugstore
dünn . . . thin
durch . . . through
durstig . . . thirsty
Dusche, die . . . shower

E

E-Zug, der . . . medium-fast train
Ecke, die . . . corner
Ei, das (die Eier) . . . egg
Eierspeisen, die . . . egg dishes
Eilzüge, die . . . medium-fast trains
ein . . . a
ein bißchen . . . a little
ein paar . . . a pair, a couple
eine . . . a
einem . . . a
einen . . . a
einer . . . a, of a
eines . . . a, of a
einfach . . . one-way, simple
Einfahrt, die . . . entrance (for vehicles)
Eingang, der . . . entrance (for people)
einhängen . . . to hang up
einlöst/einlösen . . . redeems/to redeem
Einpfennigstück, das . . one-pfennig piece
eins . . . one
einsteigen . . . to get in, board
einstempeln . . . to cancel, punch
einwerfen . . . to throw in
Eis, das . . . ice cream
Eisbecher mit Früchten, der . . ice-cream cup with fruit
Elefant, der . . . elephant
elf . . . eleven
Eltern, die . . . parents
Entschuldigung . . . excuse me
er . . . he
Erdgeschoß, das . . . ground floor
erste Klasse . . . first class
es . . . it
es gibt . . . there is, there are
es tut mir leid . . . I am sorry
essen . . . to eat
Essen, das . . . meal
Eßzimmer, das . . . dining room
Etage, die . . . floor, story
Europa, das . . . Europe
europäisch . . . European
evangelisch . . . Protestant

F

fahren . . . to go, drive, travel
Fahrenheit, die . . . Fahrenheit
Fahrkarte, die . . . ticket
Fahrplan, der . . . timetable
Fahrrad, das . . . bicycle
Fahrstuhl, der . . . elevator
Fahrt, die . . . ride, drive, trip
Farbe, die (die Farben) . . . color
Februar, der . . . February
Feinkostgeschäft, das . . . delicatessen
Fenster, das . . . window

Ferngespräch, das (die Ferngespräche) . . . . long-distance telephone call
Fernseher, der . . . . television set
Fernsprecher, der . . . . telephone
Fernsprechverzeichnis, das . . . telephone book
Fernsprechzelle, die . . . . telephone booth
Fertige Gerichte, die . . . . entrees
Feuer, das . . . . fire
Film, der (die Filme) . . . . film
finden . . . . to find
Firma, die . . . . firm, company
Fisch, der . . . . fish
Fischgerichte, die . . . . fish entrees
Fischhandlung, die . . . . fish store
Flasche, die (die Flaschen) . . . . bottle
Fleisch, das . . . . meat
fliegen . . . . to fly
Flughafen, der . . . . airport
Flugkarte, die . . . . airplane ticket
Flugreise, die . . . . airplane trip
Flugzeug, das . . . . airplane
Formular, das . . . . form
Fotogeschäft, das . . . . photo shop
Frage, die (die Fragen) . . . . question
fragen . . . . to ask
Frau, die (die Frauen) . . . . . woman, Mrs.
Fräulein, das . . . . young lady, Miss
frei . . . . free of charge, available
Freitag, der . . . . Friday
Fremdenverkehrsamt, das . . . . . . tourist office
friert/friern . . . . freezes/to freeze
frisch . . . . fresh
Friseur, der . . . . hairdresser
Frühling, der . . . . spring
Frühstück, das . . . . breakfast
Frühstücksportion, die . . . . . . breakfast portion
fünf . . . . five
Fünfhundertmarkschein, der . 500-mark bill
Fünfmarkschein, der . . . . 5-mark bill
Fünfmarkstück, das . . . . 5-mark coin
Fünfpfennigstück, das . . . 5-pfennig coin
fünfzehn . . . . fifteen
fünfzig . . . . fifty
Fünfzigmarkschein, der . . . . 50-mark bill
Fünfzigpfennigstück, das . . . 50-pfennig coin
Fundbüro, das . . . . . lost-and-found office
für . . . . for

G

g'suffa . . . . drink
Gabel, die . . . . fork
Garage, die . . . . garage
Garten, der . . . . garden, yard
Gasthaus, das . . . . restaurant, inn
Gasthof, der . . . . hotel, inn
gebacken . . . . baked
gebraten . . . . roasted, fried
Geflügel, das . . . . poultry
gegrillt . . . . grilled
geht/gehen . . . . goes/to go
gekocht . . . . cooked, boiled
gekochtes Ei . . . . boiled egg
gelb . . . . yellow
Geld, das . . . . money
Geldscheine, die . . . . bank notes
Geldstücke, die . . . . coins
gemischter Salat . . . . mixed salad
gemischtes Eis . . . . mixed ice cream
Gemüse, das . . . . vegetables
Gemüsegeschäft, das . . . vegetable store
genau . . . . exactly
genau so . . . . just as
genug . . . . enough
geradeaus . . . . straight ahead
Geschäft, das (die Geschäfte) . . . . . store
Gespräch, das . . . . conversation
gestern . . . . yesterday
gesund . . . . healthy
Glas, das . . . . glass
Gleis, das . . . . track
Glück, das . . . . luck
Goethe Museum, das . . . Goethe Museum
Grad, der . . . . degree
Gras, das . . . . grass
grau . . . . gray
Grill- und Pfannengerichte, die . . . . grilled and fried entrees
groß . . . . large
Größe, die . . . . size
Großeltern, die . . . . grandparents
Großmutter, die . . . . grandmother
Großvater, der . . . . grandfather
grün . . . . green
gut, gutes, gute . . . . good

H

Haar, das . . . . hair
haben . . . . to have
halb . . . . half
hallo . . . . hello
Haltestelle, die . . . . . transportation stop
Hammel, der . . . . mutton
Hand, die . . . . hand
Handapparat, der . . . . telephone receiver
Handschuhe, die . . . . gloves
Handtasche, die . . . . purse
Handtuch, das . . . . hand towel
hat/haben . . . . has/to have
Hat's geschmeckt? . . . . Did it taste good?
Hauptausgang, der . . . . main exit
Hauptbahnhof, der . . . main train station
Haupteingang, der . . . . . . main entrance
Haus, das . . . . house
Hausschuhe, die . . . . slippers
Hbf . . . . abbre. for main train station
heiß . . . . hot
heißt/heißen . . . . . . is called/to be called
Hemd, das (die Hemden) . . . . shirt
Herbst, der . . . . fall
Herr, der (die Herren) . . . gentleman, Mr.
Herr Ober! . . . . Waiter!
Herrenhemd, das . . . . man's shirt
heute . . . . today
hier . . . . here
hin und zurück . . . . there and back
hinter . . . . behind
hoch . . . . high
Hofbräuhaus, das . . . . brewery
Hose, die . . . . trousers
Hotel, das . . . . hotel
Hotelmanager, der . . . . . . hotel manager
Hotelrechnung, die . . . . hotel bill
Hotelzimmer, das . . . . hotel room
Hund, der . . . . dog
hundert . . . . hundred
Hundertmarkschein, der . . 100-mark bill
hungrig . . . . hungry
Hut, der . . . . hat

I

ich I
Idee, die . . . . idea
Ihnen . . . . to you
Ihr, Ihre, Ihrem . . . . your
im (= in dem) . . . . in, in the
in . . . . in
Information, die . . . . information
inland . . . . inland, domestic
Inter-City Züge, die . . . . inter-city trains
ist/sein . . . . is/to be

J

ja . . . . yes
Jacke, die . . . . jacket
Jahr, das (die Jahre) . . . . year
Januar, der . . . . January
jüdisch . . . . Jewish
Juli, der . . . . July
jung . . . . young
Juni, der . . . . June

K

Kabine, die . . . . booth
Kaffee und Kuchen . . . . . coffee and cake
Kaffee, der . . . . coffee
Kakao, der . . . . cocoa
Kalb, das . . . . veal
Kalender, der . . . . calendar
kalt . . . . cold
kalte Speisen . . . . cold meals
Kamera, die . . . . camera
Kamm, der . . . . comb
kann/können . . . . can/to be able to
Kännchen, das . . . . pot
Karte, die (die Karten) . .card, ticket, map
Kartoffeln, die . . . . potatoes
Käse, der . . . . cheese
katholisch . . . . Catholic
Katze, die . . . . cat
kauft/kaufen . . . . buys/to buy
kein Ausgang . . . . no exit
kein Eingang . . . . no entrance
Keller, der . . . . cellar
Kellner, der . . . . waiter
Kellnerin, die . . . . waitress
Kilometer, der . . . . kilometer
Kind, das (die Kinder) . . . . child
Kinderteller, der . . . . children's plate
Kino, das . . . . movie theater
Kiosk, der . . . . newsstand
Kirche, die . . . . church
Kleid, das . . . . dress
Kleider, die . . . . clothes
Kleiderschrank, der . . . . . . clothes closet
klein, kleines . . . . small
Kleingeld, das . . . . . . small change, coins
Klingel, die . . . . doorbell
kocht/kochen . . . . cooks/to cook
Koffer, der . . . . suitcase
kommt/kommen . . . . comes/to come
Konditorei, die . . . . café
können . . . . to be able to, can
Konversation, die . . . . conversation
Konzert, das . . . . concert
Konzertkarte, die . . . . concert ticket
Kopfkissen, das . . . . pillow
kostet/kosten . . . . costs
Kotelett, das . . . . cutlet, chop
krank . . . . sick, ill
Krawatte, die . . . . tie
Kreis, der . . . . circle, district
Küche, die . . . . kitchen
kühl . . . . cool
Kühlschrank, der . . . . refrigerator
Kuli, der . . . . pen
kurz . . . . short

L

Laden, der (die Läden) . . . . . . store, shop
Lampe, die (die Lampen) . . . . lamp
landen . . . . to land
Landkarte, die . . . . map
lang . . . . long
langsam . . . . slow
langsamer . . . . slower
laut . . . . loud
Lebensmittelgeschäft, das . . . . . grocery store
leise . . . . soft
lernen . . . . to learn
lesen . . . . to read
Leute, die . . . . people

Licht, das .... light
Liegewagen, der .... reclining car
Likör, der .... liqueur
Linie, die (die Linien) .... line
linken .... left
links .... left
Liste, die .... list
Liter, der .... liter
Löffel, der .... spoon
los .... wrong

M

macht/machen ...... makes/to make do
Mai, der .... May
man .... one
Mann, der .... man
Männer, die .... men
Mantel, der .... coat
Mark, die .... mark
Markstück, das .... mark piece
Markt, der .... market
Marktplatz, der .... market place
Marmelade, die .... jam
März, der .... March
mehr .... more
meine .... mine
Menü, das .... menu
Messer, das .... knife
Meter, der .... meter
Metzgerei, die .... butcher shop
Milch, die .... milk
Milchgeschäft, das .... dairy
mindestens .... at least
Mineralwasser, das ...... mineral water
Minute, die (die Minuten) .... minute
mir .... to me, me
mit .... with
Mittagessen, das .... lunch
Mitte, die .... middle
Mittwoch, der .... Wednesday
möchte/möchten .... would like
Moment, der .... moment
Monat, der (die Monate) .... month
Montag, der .... Monday
morgen .... tomorrow
Morgen, der .... morning
morgens .... mornings
Münzfernsprecher, der ... coin-operated telephone
Museum, das .... museum
Museumplatz, der ...... museum square
muß/müssen .... must/to have to
müssen .... to have to, must
Mutter, die .... mother

N

nach .... to, after
Nachmittag, der .... afternoon
nachmittags .... afternoons
Nachspeise, die .... dessert
nächst, nächsten .... next
Nacht, die .... night
Nachthemd, das .... nightshirt
Nachtisch, der .... dessert
Name, der (die Namen) .... name
neben .... next to
neblig .... foggy
nehmen .... to take
nein .... no
neu, neue, neuen .... new
neun .... nine
neunzehn .... nineteen
neunzig .... ninety
nicht .... no, not
nicht Raucher .... non-smoker
nicht wahr? .... isn't it so?
nichts .... nothing
niedrig .... low
noch .... still
Nord, der .... north

Norden, der .... north
nördlich .... northern
Notausgang, der .... emergency exit
November, der .... November
null .... zero
Nummer, die (die Nummern) .... number
nun .... now
nur .... only

O

oben .... above, upstairs
Obst, das .... fruit
Obstgeschäft, das .... fruit store
oder .... or
Ofen, der .... oven
offen .... open
öffnen .... to open
oft .... often
Oktober, der .... October
Omelett, das (die Omeletten) .. omelette
Onkel, der .... uncle
Oper, die .... opera
Opernhaus, das .... opera house
Orangensaft, der .... orange juice
Ortsgespräch, das ...... local phone call
Ost, der .... east
Osten, der .... east
östlich .... eastern

P

packen .... to pack
Paket, das .... package
paniert .... breaded
Papier, das .... paper
Papierkorb, der ..... wastepaper basket
Parkplatz, der .... parking space
parkt/parken .... parks/to park
Parterre, das .... ground floor
Paß, der .... passport
paßt/passen .... fits/to fit
Pension, die .. bed-and-breakfast lodging
Pensionzimmer, das .... room at a bed-and-breakfast
Personen, die .... persons
Personenzüge, die .... local trains
Pfeffer, der .... pepper
Pfennig, der (die Pfennige) ..... pfennig
Pfund, das .... pound
Philosophie, die .... philosophy
Photo, das .... photograph
Platz, der .... space, place
Polizei, die .... police
Polizeiamt, das .... police station
Portion, die .... portion
Post, die .... mail
Postamt, das .... post office
Postkarte, die .... postcard
Preis, der (die Preisen) .... price
pro Stunde .... per hour
Problem, das (die Probleme) ... problem
Pulli, der (die Pullis) .... sweater
purpur .... purple

Q

Quelle, die .... source
Quittung, die .... receipt

R

R-Gespräch, das .... collect call
Rathaus, das .... city hall
Ratskeller, der ...... city-hall restaurant
rauchen .... to smoke
Rauchen verboten ... smoking prohibited
Rasiermesser, das .... razor
Rechnung, die .... bill
rechten .... right
rechts .... right
Regenmantel, der .... raincoat
Regenschirm, der .... umbrella

regnet/regnen .... rains/to rain
reich .... rich
reinigt/reinigen .... cleans/to clean
Reinigung, die .... cleaners
Reise, die .... trip, travel
Reiseauskunft, die ... travel information
Reisebüro, das .... travel office
Reisekoffer, der .... trunk
reisen .... to travel
Reisewörter, die .... travel words
Religion, die (die Religionen) ... religion
Restaurant, das .... restaurant
Rettungsdienst, der ..... rescue service
richtig, richtigen .... correct
Rind, das .... beef
Ritter, der .... knight
Rock, der .... skirt
Rolltreppe, die .... escalator
rosa .... pink
Rose, die (die Rosen) .... rose
rot .... red
Rotwein, der .... red wine

S

S-Bahn, die .... streetcar
sagt/sagen .... says/to say
Sahne, die .... whipped cream, cream
Salat, der (die Salate) .... salad
Salz, das .... salt
Samstag, der .... Saturday
Sandalen, die .... sandals
sauber .... clean
sauer .... sour
Schaffner, der .... conductor
Schalter, der .... counter
Scheck, der .... check
Schein, der (die Scheine) ..... bank note
Schiff, das .... ship
Schinken, der .... ham
Schlafanzug, der .... pajamas
schlafen .... to sleep
Schlafwagen, der .... sleeping car
Schlafzimmer, das .... bedroom
schlecht .... bad
schließen .... to close
Schloß, das .... castle
Schneider, der .... tailor
schneidet/schneiden .... cuts/to cut
schneit/schneien .... snows/to snow
schnell .... fast
Schnellimbiß, der .... quick refreshment bar
Schnellzug, der .... train
Schokolade, die .... chocolate
schön .... pretty
Schrank, der .... closet, cupboard
schreiben .... to write
Schreibtisch, der .... desk
Schreibwarenhandlung, die .... stationery store
Schuh, der (die Schuhe) .... shoe
schwarz .... black
Schwein, das .... pig, pork
Schweinekotelett, das .... pork chop
Schwester, die .... sister
Schwimmbad, das ...... swimming pool
schwimmen .... to swim
sechs .... six
sechzehn .... sixteen
sechzig .... sixty
See, die .... sea
Seeblick, der .... sea view
Seereise, die .... ocean voyage
sehen .... to see
sehr .... very
Seife, die .... soap
Seite, die (die Seiten) .... page
Sekunde, die .... second
senden .... to send

September, der .... September
Serviette, die .... napkin
sie .... she, they
Sie .... you
sieben .... seven
siebzehn .... seventeen
siebzig .... seventy
sieht .... sees
sind / sein .... are / to be
singen .... to sing
sitzen .... to sit
so .... as
Socken, die .... socks
Sofa, das .... sofa
Sohn, der .... son
Sommer, der .... summer
Sonnenbrille, die .... sunglasses
Sonntag, der .... Sunday
Spanien, das .... Spain
Spanisch, das .... Spanish
spät .... late
später .... later
Speisekarte, die .... menu
Speisewagen, der .... dining car
Spezialität, die .... specialty
Spiegel, der .... mirror
Sport, der .... sport
sprechen .... to speak
Stadt, die (die Städte) .... city
Stadtmitte, die .... city center
Stadtplan, der .... city map
Stammbaum, der .... family tree
steht / stehen .... stands / to stand
steigen .... to climb
Stiefel, die .... boots
Stock, das .... floor
Straße, die .... street
Straßenbahn, die .... streetcar
Straßenbahnhaltestelle, die ... streetcar stop
Straßenschilder, die .... street signs
Strumpfe, die .... socks
Strumpfhose, die .... panty hose
Stück, das .... piece
Stuhl, der (die Stühle) .... chair
Stunde, die (die Stunden) .... hour
Süd .... south
Süden, der .... south
südlich .... southern
Suppe, die (die Suppen) .... soup
süß .... sweet
Süßwarenladen, der .... candy shop

T

Tabak, der .... tobacco
Tabakladen, der .... tobacco store
Tag, der (die Tage) .... day
Tagesgericht, das .... daily special
Tankstelle, die .... gas station
Tante, die .... aunt
Taschentuch, das .... handkerchief
Tasse, die (die Tassen) .... cup
tausend .... thousand
Tausendmarkschein, der . thousand-mark bill
Taxi, das .... taxi
TEE ..... Trans-European Express train
Tee, der .... tea
Telefon, das .... telephone
Telefonanruf, der .... telephone call
Telefonbuch, das .... telephone book
Telefongespräch, das ..... telephone call
telefonieren .... to telephone
Telefonnummer, die .. telephone number
Telefonzelle, die .... telephone booth
Telegramm, das .... telegram
Teller, der .... plate
Temperatur, die .... temperature
Teppich, der .... carpet
teuer .... expensive
Theater, das .... theater
Theaterkarte, ... theater ticket
Tisch, der (die Tische) .... table
Toast, der .... toast
Tochter, die .... daughter
Toilette, die .... lavatory
Tomatensaft, der .... tomato juice
Tourist, der .... tourist
Treppe, die .... steps
trinken .... to drink
Tür, die .... door
typisch, typische .... typical

U

U-Bahn, die (die U-Bahnen) .... subway
U-Bahnfahrplan, der ... subway schedule
U-Bahnhaltestelle, die .... subway shop
über .... over, above
Überfall, der .... attack, accident
Uhr, die (die Uhren) .... clock, watch
Uhrmacher, der .... watchmaker
um .... around, at
umsteigen .... to transfer
und .... and
ungefähr .... approximately
uninteressant .... uninteresting
Universität, die .... university
unten .... below, downstairs
unter .... under
Unterhemd, das .... undershirt
Unterhose, die .... underpants
Unterrock, der .... slip

V

Vater, der .... father
Verb, das (die Verben) .... verb
verbinden .... to connect
verboten .... prohibited
Vereinigten Staaten, die .... the United States
vergessen .... to forget
verkaufen .... to sell
Verkehrsunfall, der ..... traffic accident
verlieren .... to lose
versch. .... abbre. for various
verstehen .... to understand
Verwandten, die .... relatives
viel .... much
viel Spaß .... much fun
viele .... many
vier .... four
Viertel, das .... quarter
vierzehn .... fourteen
vierzig .... forty
violett .... violet
voll .... full, drunk
vom (= von dem) .... from the
vom Hammel .... mutton
vom Kalb .... veal
vom Rind .... beef
vom Schwein .... pork
von .... from
vor .... in front of
Vorhang, der .... curtain
Vorname, der .... first name
vorsichtig .... careful
Vorspeisen, die .... hors d'oeuvres
Vorwahlnummer, die ... telephone prefix

W

Wagen, der .... car
wählen .... to dial
Wahlton, der .... dial tone
Wand, die .... wall
wann .... when
war .... was
Waren, die .... wares
Warenhaus, das ...... department store
warm .... warm
Wartesaal, der .... waiting room
warum .... why
was .... what
Waschbecken, das .... sink
waschen .... to wash
Wäscherei, die .... laundry
Waschlappen, der .... washcloth
wäscht / waschen ...... washes / to wash
Wasser, das .... water
Wechselstube, die. money-exchange office
wechselt / wechseln ...... exchanges / to exchange
Wecker, der .... alarm clock
Wein, der .... wine
Weinstube, die .... wine cellar
weiß / wissen .... knows / to know
weiß .... white
Weißwein, der .... white wine
weiter .... further
welche, welches, welchem .... which
wenig .... few
wer .... who
West, der .... west
Westen, der .... west
westlich .... western
Wetter, das .... weather
wichtig, wichtige .... important
wie .... how
Wie geht's? .... How are you?
wie lange .... how long
wieder .... again
wiederholen .... to repeat
wieviel .... how much
Wild, das .... venison
windig .... windy
Winter, der .... winter
wir .... we
wissen .... to know (a fact)
wo .... where
Woche, die (die Wochen) .... week
wohnen .... to live, reside
Wohnzimmer, das .... living room
Wort, das (die Wörter) .... word
Wörterbuch, das .... dictionary
Wurst, die .... sausage

Z

zahlen .... to pay
Zahnbürste, die .... toothbrush
Zahnpaste, die .... toothpaste
zehn .... ten
Zehnmarkschein, der ..... ten-mark bill
Zehnpfennigstück, das . ten-pfennig coin
Zentimeter, der .... centimeter
zeigen .... to show
Zeit, die .... time
Zeitschrift, die .... magazine
Zeitung, die .... newspaper
Zentrum, das .... center (of a city)
Zigarette, die .... cigarette
Zimmer, das .... room
Zoll, der .... customs
Zoo, der .... zoo
zu .... to, closed
Zug, der (die Züge) .... train
Zugfahrplan, der .... train schedule
Zugkarte, die .... train ticket
Zugreise, die .... train trip
zum (= zu dem) .... to the
zur (= zu der) .... to the
zur Sonne .... at the sun
zwanzig .... twenty
Zwanzigmarkschein, der .. twenty-mark bill
zwei .... two
Zweimarkstück, das ..... two-mark coin
Zweipfennigstück, das . two-pfennig coin
zweite Klasse .... second class
zwölf .... twelve

DRINKING GUIDE

This drinking guide is intended to explain the sometimes overwhelming variety of beverages available to you while in Germany. It is by no means complete. Some of the experimenting has been left up to you, but this should get you started. The asterisks (*) indicate brand names.

HEIßE GETRÄNKE (hot drinks)

Tasse Kaffee .... cup of coffee
Portion/Kännchen Kaffee ...... pot of coffee
Glas Tee .... cup of tea
(schwarz, Kamille) .... (black, camomile)
Portion/Kännchen Tee .... pot of tea
mit Zitrone .... with lemon
mit Sahne .... with cream
Glühwein .... hot red wine with spices
Grog vom Rum .... grog from rum

ALKOHOLFREIE GETRÄNKE (non-alcoholic drinks)

Fanta .... Fanta
Cola .... cola
Ginger Ale .... ginger ale
Soda .... club soda
Tonic Water .... tonic water
Bitter Lemon .... bitter lemon
Spezi .... 1/2 cola, 1/2 Fanta
Apfelsaft .... apple juice
Orangensaft .... orange juice
Tomatensaft .... tomato juice
Traubensaft weiß .... white grape juice
Johannisbeersaft schwarz ..... black currant juice
Milch .... milk
Buttermilch .... buttermilk
Orangenlimonade .... orange drink
Zitronenlimonade .... lemon-flavored drink
Mineralwasser .... mineral water

SPIRITUOSEN (spirits)

Gin .... gin
Rum .... rum
Russischer Wodka .... Russian vodka
Echter serbischer Slivovic ... Serbian slivovic
Zwetschgenwasser .... prune schnapps
Kirschwasser .... cherry schnapps
Himbeergeist .... raspberry schnapps
Williams-Birne .... pear schnapps
***Obstler**
***Enzian**
***Doppelkorn**
***Doornkaat**

WHISKIES (whiskies)

This list has familiar names like Red Label, Black Label, Seagrams, etc. The Germans do have a clear whisky called **Korn** which is frequently ordered along with a **Bier.**

LIKÖRE (liqueurs)

Eierlikör .... egg liqueur
Aprikot Brandy .... apricot brandy
Kirschlikör .... cherry liqueur
(and various other fruit liqueurs)
***Schwarzer Kater**
***Ettaler Klosterlikör**
***Drambuie**
***Cointreau**
***Grand Marnier**

HALBBITTER UND BITTER (bitters)

***Underberg**
***Jägermeister**
***Mampe Diktiner**

BIERE (beers)

There is a variety of brands. **Bier** is purchased in **Flaschen** (bottles) or **vom Faß** (draft).

Export vom Faß .... draft export
Pils .... pilsner
Diät-Pils .... diet pilsner
Altbier .... dark beer
Weizenbier .... special wheat beer
Berliner Weiße .... Berlin specialty — beer
(mit oder ohne Schuß-Waldmeister oder Himbeersirup) (with or without a shot of **Waldmeister** or raspberry syrup)

WEINE (wines)

There are three main types and quality levels. **Wein** is purchased by the **Flasche** (bottle) or **offen** (open, like a house wine).

Rotwein .... red wine
Weißwein .... white wine
Rosé .... rosé

Tafelwein .... table wine
Qualitätswein .... quality wine
Kabinettwein .... choice wine
Eiswein .... rare, special ice wine

Schorle .... wine mixed with mineral water

The major wine-producing areas in **Deutschland** are

Baden **Rheinhessen**
Mosel **Neckar**
Rhein **Franken**

APÊRITIFS UND SÜDWEINE (aperitifs)

Sherry .... sherry
Portwein .... port
***Pernod**
***Campari**
***Martini weiß** (Not gin with an olive, but sweet vermouth!
***Martini rot** If you order a "martini," this is what you will get.)

COGNAC UND WEINBRAND (cognac)

***Remy Martin**
***Asbach Uralt**

SEKT UND CHAMPAGNER (champagne)

***Henkel**
***Kupferberg**

GUT IM SOMMER

Erdbeerbowle .... champagne, white wine, strawberries
Pfirsischbowle .... champagne, white wine, peaches

GUT IM WINTER

Feuerzangenbowle .... red wine, orange slices, spices, sugar block coated with rum, flambé

CUT ALONG DOTTED LINE, FOLD AND TAKE WITH YOU

Brot und Teigwaren (bread and pasta)

Brötchen	roll
Roggenbrot	rye bread
Schwarzbrot	Westphalian brown bread
Weißbrot	white bread
Nudeln	noodles
Spätzle	dumpling

Salate (salads)

Kopfsalat	lettuce
Bohnensalat	bean salad
Gemüsesalat	vegetable salad
Feldsalat	lamb's salad
Tomatensalat	tomato salad
Kartoffelsalat	potato salad
Endiviensalat	endive salad
Gurkensalat	cucumber salad
Selleriesalat	celery salad
Chikoreesalat	chicory salad
gemischter Salat	mixed salad
Geflügelsalat	chicken salad

Gemüse (vegetables)

Bohnen	beans
Erbsen	peas
Linsen	lentils
Spargel	asparagus
Karotten	carrots
Spinat	spinach
Lauch	leek
Tomaten	tomatoes
Pilze, Champignons	mushrooms
Weißkohl, Weißkraut	white cabbage
Rotkohl, Rotkraut	red cabbage
Blumenkohl	cauliflower
Rosenkohl	brussels sprouts
rote Beete, rote Rübe	beets
Mais	corn
Gurken	cucumbers
Kohlrabi	turnip-cabbage, kohlrabi
Zwiebeln	onions
Radieschen	radish (small, red kind)
Rettich	radish (big, white root)
Meerrettich	horseradish

Kartoffeln (potatoes)

gekochte Kartoffeln, Salzkartoffeln	boiled potatoes
Bratkartoffeln, Röstkartoffeln	fried potatoes
Kartoffelgemüse	potatoes in cream sauce
Kartoffelpüree, Kartoffelbrei	mashed potatoes
Pommes Frites	French fried potatoes
Kartoffelknödel	potato dumpling
Petersilienkartoffeln	parsley potatoes

Obst (fruit)

Apfel	apple
Birne	pear
Aprikose	apricot
Pfirsich	peach
Banane	banana
Orange, Apfelsine	orange
Mandarine	tangerine
Kirsche	cherry
Pflaume, Zwetschge	plum
Mirabelle	sweet, yellow plum
Apfelmus	applesauce
Kürbis	pumpkin
Melone	melon
Pampelmuse, Grapefruit	grapefruit
Kompott	stewed fruit
Traube	grape

Beeren (berries)

Erdbeere	strawberry
Himbeere	raspberry
Brombeere	blackberry
Stachelbeere	gooseberry
Johannisbeere (rot oder schwarz)	red or black currant
Preiselbeere	cranberry, red bilberry
Heidelbeere	blueberry

Guten Appetit!

die Speisekarte

menu

Art der Zubereitung (ways of preparation)

im Backteig	in batter
gekocht	cooked, boiled
gebraten	roasted, fried
gebacken	baked
gedämpft	steamed
geschmort	braised
gegrillt	grilled
paniert	breaded
roh - englisch	rare
kurz angebraten	medium-rare
durchgebraten	well-done

Allgemeines (general)

Marmelade	jam
Gelee	jelly
Honig	honey
Salz	salt
Pfeffer	pepper
Öl	oil
Essig	vinegar
Senf	mustard
Sosse	gravy
Aufschnitt	cold cuts
Käse	cheese
Nachtisch	dessert
Kuchen	cake
Gebäck	pastry
Eis	ice cream
Schlagsahne	whipped cream

Vorspeisen (hors d'oeuvres)

Austern	oysters
Gänseleber-Pastete	goose-liver pate
Heringsalat	herring salad
Italienischer Salat	Italian salad
Kaviar	caviar
Raucheraal	smoked eel
Russische Eier	Russian eggs
Weinbergschnecken	snails
Hummer-Cocktail	lobster cocktail
Froschschenkel	frog's legs

Suppen (soups)

Kraftbrühe mit Ei	clear soup with raw egg
Tagessuppe	soup of the day
klare Fleischbrühe	beef broth
Hühnerbrühe	chicken broth
Bohnensuppe	bean soup
Erbsensuppe	pea soup
Linsensuppe	lentil soup
Kartoffelsuppe	potato soup
Champignoncremesuppe	cream-of-mushroom soup
Ochsenschwanzsuppe	oxtail soup
Gulaschsuppe	Hungarian goulash soup
Schildkrötensuppe	turtle soup
Königinsuppe	cream-of-chicken soup

Eierspeisen (eggs)

ein weich gekochtes Ei	one soft-boiled egg
ein hart gekochtes Ei	one hard-boiled egg
Spiegelei	fried egg
Rührei	scrambled eggs
verlorenes Ei	poached egg
Omelett mit . . .	omelette with . . .
Bauernomelett	farmer's omelette
Strammer Max	open ham sandwich, fried egg on top

Fleisch (meat)

vom Kalb, Kalbfleisch (veal)

Kalbsbraten	roast veal
Kalbssteak	veal steak
Kalbsschnitzel	veal cutlet
Wiener Schnitzel	breaded veal cutlet

Fleisch (meat) continued

Paprika Schnitzel	red-pepper veal cutlet
Kalbskotelett	veal chop
Kalbsfrikassee	fricassee of veal
Kalbshaxe	shank of veal
Kalbskeule	leg of veal
gefüllte Kalbsbrust	stuffed breast of veal
Kalbsnierenbraten	loin of veal with kidneys
Kalbszunge	veal tongue
Kalbsleber	calf's liver
Kalbslendenbraten	filet of veal
Kalbsrollbraten	rolled veal roast

vom Rind (beef)

Rindfleisch-Ochsenfleisch	broiled beef
Rindersaftbraten	braised beef
Ochsenbrust	boiled brisket of beef
Lendensteak	loin steak
Deutsches Beefsteak	Salisbury steak
Gulasch	Hungarian goulash
Schmorbraten	pot roast
Ochsenzunge	beef tongue
Filetgulasch Stroganoff	beef Stroganoff
Rinderroulade	stuffed, rolled beef slices
Wiener Rostbraten	cube steak with fried onions

vom Schwein, Schweinefleisch (pork)

Schweinebraten	roast pork
Schweineschnitzel	pork steak
Schweinekotelett	pork chop
Schweinelendchen	pork filet
Schweinshaxe	pig's knuckles (fried)
Kassler Rippenspeer	saddle of pork
Schweineragout	ragout/stew
Hausmacher Bratwurst	homemade fried sausage
Eisbein	pig's knuckles (cooked)
Leberkäse	liver loaf
Schlachtplatte	hot pork sausages with sauerkraut

von Hammel, Hammelfleisch (mutton)

Hammelbraten	roast mutton
Hammelkotelett	mutton chop
Hammelkeule	leg of mutton
Lamm	lamb
Lammbraten	roast lamb

Geflügel (poultry)

Brathuhn	roast chicken
Hühnerfrikassee	chicken fricassee
Ente	duck
Gans	goose
Rebhuhn	partridge
Fasan	pheasant
Taube	pigeon
Truthahn/Puter	turkey

Wild (venison)

Hirschbraten	roast stag
Hirschsteak	steak of stag
Rehkeule	leg of roe deer
Rehbraten	roast venison
Rehlendenbraten	filet roast of venison
Hirschkeule	leg of deer
Wildschweinbraten	roast wild boar
Wildschweinsteak	wild-boar steak
Hasenkeule	leg of hare
Hasenrücken	saddle of hare
Hasenpfeffer	jugged hare

Fisch (fish)

Schellfisch	haddock
Scholle (Flunder)	flounder
Heilbutt	halibut
Forelle	trout (boiled/fried)
Goldbarschfilet	bass filet
Kabeljau	cod
Seezunge	sole
Makrele	mackerel
Hecht	pike
Muscheln	mussels
Krebse	crab
Krebsschwänze	freshwater shrimps
Karpfen	carp
Krabben	small shrimps
Ölsardinen	sardines (in oil)
Salm	salmon
Lachs/Raucherlachs	salmon/smoked salmon
Sardellen	anchovies
Aal	eel

(koh-men) **kommen**	*(high-sen)* **heißen**
(gay-en) **gehen**	*(kow-fen)* **kaufen**
(hah-ben) **haben**	*(shprek-en)* **sprechen**
(lair-nen) **lernen**	*(voh-nen)* **wohnen**
(murk-ten) **möchten**	*(be-stel-en)* **bestellen**
(brow-ken) **brauchen**	*(bly-ben)* **bleiben**

to be called

to come

to buy

to go

to speak

to have

to live/reside

to learn

to order

would like

to stay/remain

to need

(zah-gen) **sagen**	*(fair-kow-fen)* **verkaufen**
(es-sen) **essen**	*(zeh-en)* **sehen**
(trink-en) **trinken**	*(zen-den)* **senden**
(shtay-en) **stehen**	*(shlah-fen)* **schlafen**
(fair-shtay-en) **verstehen**	*(fin-den)* **finden**
(vee-dair-hoh-len) **wiederholen**	*(mah-ken)* **machen**

to sell

to say

to see

to eat

to send

to drink

to sleep

to stand

to find

to understand

to do/make

to repeat

(shry-ben) **schreiben**	*(lay-zen)* **lesen**
(tsigh-gen) **zeigen**	*(fahr-en)* **fahren**
(be-tsah-len) *(tsah-len)* **bezahlen/zahlen**	*(ar-by-ten)* **arbeiten**
(kur-nen) **können**	*(flee-gen)* **fliegen**
(mew-sen) **müssen**	*(zit-zen)* **sitzen**
(viss-en) **wissen**	*(pahk-en)* **packen**

to read

to write

to drive/travel

to show

to work

to pay

to fly

to be able to/can

to sit

to have to/must

to pack

to know

(bay-ginn-en) **beginnen**	*(bring-en)* **bringen**
(urf-nen) **öffnen**	*(shtai-gen)* **steigen**
(kohk-hen) **kochen**	*(ows-shtai-gen)* **aussteigen**
(lahn-den) **landen**	*(ine-shtai-gen)* **einsteigen**
(booh-ken) **buchen**	*(oom-shtai-gen)* **umsteigen**
(koh-sten) **kosten**	*(on-koh-men)* **ankommen**

to bring

to begin

to climb

to open

to get out

to cook

to get in

to land

to transfer

to book/reserve

to arrive

to cost

(ahp-fahr-en)
abfahren

(shlee-sen)
schließen

(ry-zen)
reisen

(vah-shen)
waschen

(rau-ken)
rauchen

(vex-zeln)
wechseln

(frah-gen)
fragen

(fair-lear-en)
verlieren

(es) (shnait)
es schneit

(eehk) (bin)
ich bin

(es) (rayg-net)
es regnet

(vir) (zint)
wir sind

to close

to depart

to wash

to travel

to exchange

to smoke

to lose

to ask

I am

it is snowing

we are

it is raining

(air) **er** (zee) **sie** (es) **es** } **ist**	(hohk) **hoch** - (nee-drig) **niedrig**
(zee) **Sie** (zint) **sind**	(ahrm) **arm** - (rike) **reich**
(zee) **sie** (zint) **sind**	(koorts) **kurz** - (long) **lang**
(owf) **Auf** (vee-dair-zeh-en) **Wiedersehen!**	(krahnk) **krank** - (ge-zoont) **gesund**
(es) **es** (gipt) **gibt**	(bil-ig) **billig** - (toy-air) **teuer**
(vee) **Wie** (gate) **geht** (es) **es** (ee-nen) **Ihnen?**	(ahlt) **alt** - (yoong) **jung**

high - low

he
she
it } is

poor - rich

you are

short - long

they are

sick - healthy

good-bye

cheap - expensive

there is/there are

old - young

How are you?

(goot) **gut** - *(shleckt)* **schlecht**	*(shnel)* **schnell** - *(long-zahm)* **langsam**
(ly-zah) **leise** - *(laut)* **laut**	*(dick)* **dick** - *(dewn)* **dünn**
(gross) **groß** - *(kline)* **klein**	*(feel)* **viel** - *(vay-nig)* **wenig**
(hice) **heiß** - *(kahlt)* **kalt**	*(owf)* **auf** - *(tsoo)* **zu**
(links) **links** - *(rex)* **rechts**	*(zeus)* **süß** - *(zow-air)* **sauer**
(oh-ben) **oben** - *(oon-ten)* **unten**	*(ent-shool-dee-goong)* **Entschuldigung!**

fast - slow

good - bad

thick - thin

soft - loud

much - little

large - small

open - closed

hot - cold

sweet - sour

left - right

excuse me

above - below

low that you've finished...

'ou've done it!

'ou've completed all 23 Steps, stuck your abels, flashed your cards and clipped your nenu. Do you realize how far you've come ınd how much you've learned? In a short ›eriod of time, you have accomplished what it ›ometimes takes years to achieve in a tradiional language class.

'ou can now confidently

- ask questions,
- understand directions,
- make reservations,
- order food and
- shop anywhere.

\nd you can do it all in a foreign language! This means you can now go anywhere - from a arge cosmopolitan restaurant to a small, outof-the-way village where no one speaks English. Your experiences will be much more enjoyable and worry-free now that you speak he language, understand what is being said and know something of the culture.

'es, learning a foreign language can be fun. And no, not everyone abroad speaks English.

Kristine Kershul

Have a wonderful time, whether your trip is to Europe, the Orient or simply across the border.

REORDER FORM

Please send me the following titles from the series.

Title	Quantity	Price Each	Total
CHINESE		US $12.95	
FRENCH		US $12.95	
GERMAN		US $12.95	
INGLES		US $12.95	
ITALIAN		US $12.95	
JAPANESE		US $12.95	
NORWEGIAN		US $12.95	
RUSSIAN		US $12.95	
SPANISH		US $12.95	
PREFERRED READER	Sub-total		
	WA residents add tax		
	Total Order		

PLEASE CHECK:

☐ Bill my credit card account ☐ VISA ☐ MC ☐ AMEX

no.__________ exp. date_____/_____

☐ My check for $__________ is enclosed.

Name __________

Address __________

City__________ State_____ Zip_____

Telephone No. (____)__________

REORDER FORM

Please send me the following titles from the series.

Title	Quantity	Price Each	Total
CHINESE		US $12.95	
FRENCH		US $12.95	
GERMAN		US $12.95	
INGLES		US $12.95	
ITALIAN		US $12.95	
JAPANESE		US $12.95	
NORWEGIAN		US $12.95	
RUSSIAN		US $12.95	
SPANISH		US $12.95	
PREFERRED READER	Sub-total		
	WA residents add tax		
	Total Order		

PLEASE CHECK:

☐ Bill my credit card account ☐ VISA ☐ MC ☐ AMEX

no.__________ exp. date_____/_____

☐ My check for $__________ is enclosed.

Name __________

Address __________

City__________ State_____ Zip_____

Telephone No. (____)__________

Coming soon...

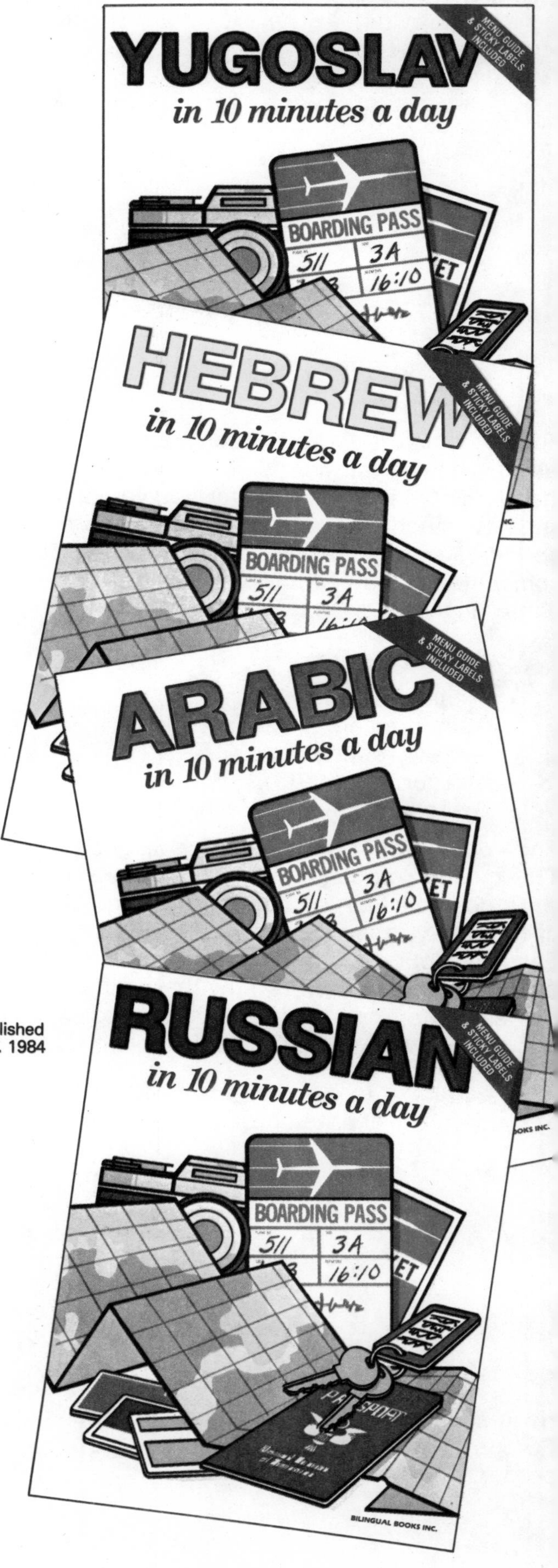

YUGOSLAV *in 10 minutes a day*

MENU GUIDE & STICKY LABELS INCLUDED

HEBREW *in 10 minutes a day*

MENU GUIDE & STICKY LABELS INCLUDED

ARABIC *in 10 minutes a day*

MENU GUIDE & STICKY LABELS INCLUDED

RUSSIAN *in 10 minutes a day*

MENU GUIDE & STICKY LABELS INCLUDED

BILINGUAL BOOKS INC.

Published
Feb. 1984

BUSINESS REPLY MAIL

FIRST CLASS PERMIT NO. 8300 SEATTLE, WASHINGTON

POSTAGE WILL BE PAID BY ADDRESSEE

BILINGUAL BOOKS INC.

5903 Seaview Avenue N.W.
Seattle, Washington 98107

NO POSTAGE NECESSARY IF MAILED IN THE UNITED STATES